GOOD EATING

ONE–DISH MEALS

GOOD EATING

ONE-DISH MEALS

YOUR COMPLETE GUIDE TO COOKING PERFECT ONE-DISH MEALS EVERY TIME

This edition published in 2011

LOVE FOOD is an imprint of Parragon Books Ltd

Parragon
Queen Street House
4 Queen Street
Bath BA1 1HE, UK

ISBN 978-1-4454-3956-3

Printed in China

Cover design by Talking Design
Photography by Mike Cooper
Food styling by Sumi Glass and Lincoln Jefferson
Introduction by Christine McFadden

This book uses imperial, metric, and US cup measurements. Follow the same units of measurement throughout; do not mix imperial and metric. All spoon measurements are level: teaspoons are assumed to be 5 ml, and tablespoons are assumed to be 15 ml. Unless otherwise stated, milk is assumed to be whole, eggs and individual vegetables, such as potatoes, are medium, and pepper is freshly ground black pepper.

The times given are an approximate guide only. Preparation times differ according to the techniques used by different people and the cooking times may also vary from those given as a result of the type of oven used. Optional ingredients, variations, or serving suggestions have not been included in the calculations.

Recipes using raw or very lightly cooked eggs should be avoided by infants, the elderly, pregnant women, convalescents, and anyone with a chronic condition. Pregnant and breast-feeding women are advised to avoid eating peanuts and peanut products. People with nut allergies should be aware that some of the prepared ingredients used in the recipes in this book may contain nuts. Always check the package before use.

CONTENTS

INTRODUCTION

These days most of us lead action-packed lives, either at work or as a busy parent, or both. Time-consuming meal preparation, let alone clearing up afterward, just doesn't fit in very easily. Yet most of us care about health and want to eat nutritious home-cooked food. What could be more satisfying than something simmering on the stove, filling the air with delicious aromas?

If you love cooking but are short of time, then *The Big Book of One Pot* will be a lifesaver. As the name suggests, all the dishes can be cooked in a single pot with other ingredients, leaving you with very little to wash up but plenty of time to get on with other things.

The one-pot method is a relaxed and flexible way of cooking, easily adjusted to whatever ingredients you have in your refrigerator or pantry. If one ingredient is missing, it's usually possible to substitute another. If you're short of space or equipment, one-pot cooking is ideal— you need just one pot and a single burner.

One-pot cooking doesn't limit you to soups and stews, though this book contains plenty of recipes for these. In many parts of the world, cooking in a single pot is the norm, whether it's a cauldron, a wok, a tagine, or a bean pot. Many dishes grew up out of necessity when food and fuel were scarce. Others were created for religious reasons—the Muslim Ramadan, for example, or the Jewish Sabbath when orthodox believers are forbidden to work or cook. The pot could be left to simmer slowly overnight ready to serve at sunset the following day. In cold climates, it was the conviviality and friendship of communal eating that inspired many one-pot dishes. Think of Swiss fondue, Hungarian goulash, or Mongolian hot pot.

As the recipes in the book demonstrate, this no-frills way of cooking is the ultimate in convenience since everything is ready at the same time. It's the ideal food for solitary suppers or for feeding a crowd. Just put the pot on the table and tuck in.

GETTING STARTED

Although one-pot cooking appears simple, it relies on a certain amount of preplanning to ensure that things go smoothly. More importantly, getting organized from the start means you can relax and enjoy the actual process of cooking instead of running around the kitchen looking for missing utensils or, worse still, discovering too late that you've run out of a vital ingredient.

Before you start to cook:

- Read the recipe all the way through, then plan the sequence according to what needs soaking, chopping, precooking, and so on.
- Have the right tools and cookware at hand
- Make sure knives are sharp
- Wash fresh vegetables, fruits, and herbs
- Assemble all the ingredients then measure or weigh them as necessary
- Complete any preparation beforehand, such as chopping or grating
- Have the prepared ingredients lined up in bowls, ready to add to the pot at the correct time
- Clear up as you go along

USEFUL UTENSILS

As well as basics such as knives and cutting boards, there are a number of additional utensils that make one-pot cooking easier and safer.

Though you can happily leave the pot to simmer while you get on with something else, it's still important to keep track of temperature and time. Thermometers are essential for food safety, and a timer with a loud ring is invaluable for reminding you when the dish needs your attention. You'll also need spoons and spatulas for stirring, and tools for turning and lifting ingredients that are precooked in stages before they go into the pot. A sturdy long-handled fork or multipronged meat lifter are handy for large pieces of meat, while stainless steel spring-action tongs let you clasp smaller pieces of food securely. A perforated shallow skimmer is useful for removing froth and foam from the surface of stews.

Although one-pot recipes are infinitely flexible, it's worth investing in proper measuring spoons and cups, as well as a kitchen scale, especially if you are new to cooking. Once you gain experience and confidence, it's fine to add a pinch of this and a handful of that.

The joy of one-pot meals is that they can be brought straight from oven to table. However, heat can damage unprotected surfaces, so it's a good idea to have a trivet or pot stand at the ready.

COOKWARE

For most of the recipes in this book, a few heavy-bottom saucepans and casseroles in varying sizes with tight-fitting lids make up the basic equipment. You'll also need a high-sided skillet, a wok, good-quality roasting pans that won't warp or twist, and some shallow baking dishes for gratins and crumbles.

FRESH PRODUCE

Wholesome fresh vegetables, meat, poultry, and fish add valuable nutrients to one-pot meals, as well as color, texture, and appetizing flavors.

Vegetables

Vegetables are one of the most important sources of vitamins, minerals, and fiber. They are packed with carotenoids (the plant form of vitamin A), vitamin C, and vitamin E, which collectively protect against heart disease and some cancers.

Meat and poultry

Meat and poultry provide high-quality protein, important minerals such as iron and zinc, and B vitamins, which are needed to release energy from food. Meat tends to be high in fat, so if you're trying to cut down, trim off any excess or choose lean cuts.

Fish and seafood

Dense-fleshed fish and seafood make marvelous one-pot meals. They provide protein and essential minerals, while oily fish such as tuna are a unique source of omega-3 fatty acids that protect against heart disease and feed the brain.

Fresh herbs

A generous sprinkling of fresh herbs added at the end of cooking will provide delightful fragrance and color to one pot meals.

PANTRY ITEMS

A pantry judiciously stocked with a few essentials means you are never without the makings of a one-pot meal.

Grains

Grains such as rice, barley, oats, quinoa, and bulgur wheat contain a range of concentrated nutrients. Perked up with colorful spices and herbs, they form a nutritious base to which meat, fish, and vegetables can be added as necessary.

Beans

Dried beans are packed with nutrients, and provide a mellow background to more strongly flavored ingredients. Canned beans are invaluable since you can add them to the pot without soaking or precooking.

Pasta

Short pasta shapes, from tiny star shapes to coils and fat tubes, make the basis for endless one pot meals. Pasta shapes can be precooked or added to the pot with plenty of liquid.

Seeds and nuts

Crunchy seeds and nuts provide texture and, if chopped finely, can give body to the cooking liquid. Pumpkin, sunflower, and sesame seeds are particularly nutritious, as are walnuts, almonds, and Brazil nuts.

Sauces and pastes

A judicious splash of sauce or dollop of paste can perk up an otherwise bland dish. Soy sauce, Worcestershire sauce, and Tabasco all have outstanding flavors, as do tomato paste, tapenade, and mustards. Ready-made jars of ethnic sauces also add exciting flavors, and save time too.

Spices and dried herbs

For the best flavor, buy spices whole (including pepper) and grind them as needed. Rosemary, thyme, and oregano are the best herbs to use dried; the more delicate varieties are better when fresh. Add spices and dried herbs at the early stages of cooking to bring out the full flavor.

MAKING THE MOST OF THE POT

One-pot meals can be cooked in a variety of pots and pans. Knowing how to get the best from them is invaluable when tackling new recipes.

Casserole

A casserole is ideal for leisurely stews and braises cooked either on the stove or in the oven, and for pot-roasting boned and large rolled pieces of meat. Poultry thighs and drumsticks and dense-fleshed root vegetables are good too. The moist heat encourages a magical exchange of flavors between meat, vegetables, and seasonings, resulting in truly succulent dishes.

After an hour or two with the lid on, test by prodding with a skewer. Meat should feel meltingly tender and root vegetables should be soft but not disintegrating.

High-sided skillet

With a tight-fitting lid and heavy bottom, a high-sided skillet is perfect for slow-cooked rice dishes such as jambalaya, and for braising larger items like chicken quarters or chops. The generous surface area provides maximum contact with heat, enabling meat to brown quickly before adding other ingredients. The contents can then be covered and left to cook at a leisurely pace.

Wok

Given the wok's conical shape and continuous stirring, the food continually falls back to the center where the heat is at its most intense. Since the ingredients are constantly on the move, much less fat is needed, making this a healthy way of cooking.

It is very important to preheat the wok. You should be able to feel the heat radiating from it when you hold your hand flat above the bottom of the interior. Add the oil only when the wok is really hot.

It is essential to have all the ingredients prepared, ready to add to the wok the minute the oil is at the right heat. It should be almost, but not quite, smoking.

Roasting pan

A good solid roasting pan is ideal for a large piece of meat or poultry cooked alongside vegetables such as onions, potatoes, and parsnips. Orange-fleshed vegetables are particularly delicious—try carrots, pumpkin, and sweet potato. Make sure the vegetables are cut into similar-size pieces so that they cook evenly. Tuck some under the meat for extra flavor. A little stock, wine, or water is all that's needed to keep everything moist.

Some roasting pans are self-basting. They have dimpled lids that encourage moisture to gather and drip evenly over the contents below, resulting in a particularly succulent dish.

A pan that is sturdy enough to use on the stove means you can speed up the cooking by giving the meat a quick sizzle before it goes into the oven. The caramelized sediment will dissolve and flavor the other ingredients once they give up their liquid.

Baking and gratin dishes

These dishes are for food that is baked in the oven with a browned topping of potato, bubbling cheese, or crunchy breadcrumbs—or all three.

Baking dishes are particularly suitable for one-pot meals because they can be brought straight from oven to table, saving on the washing up. They are usually made in attractive shapes and colors.

TOP TIPS FOR PERFECT RESULTS

Once you have tried out a few recipes, you may want to create your own one-pot favorites. It's a good idea to follow a few basic techniques:

- Browning meat and poultry before adding other ingredients will produce an appetizing caramelized crust that will dissolve and add flavor to the rest of the dish.

- Add ingredients in descending order of cooking times, slow-cooking dense items first and quick-cooking items last. That way, your one-pot meal will have appetizing texture.

- Add green vegetables just in time to cook them. They'll keep their bright color and the flavor won't dominate the rest of the dish.

- Best of all is homemade stock, either fresh or frozen. Otherwise use Swiss vegetable bouillon powder—stock cubes can be very salty.

Beef Stock

Makes 7$\frac{1}{2}$ cups

Ingredients

2 lb 4 oz/1 kg beef marrow bones, sawn into 3-inch/7.5-cm pieces
1 lb 7 oz/650 g braising beef in a single piece
5 pints water
4 cloves
2 onions, halved
2 celery stalks, coarsely chopped
8 peppercorns
1 bouquet garni

1 Put the bones in a large, heavy pan and put the braising beef on top. Pour in the water and bring to a boil over low heat. Skim off the foam that rises to the surface.

2 Press a clove into each onion half and add to the pan with the celery, peppercorns, and bouquet garni. Partially cover and simmer gently for 3 hours. Remove the stewing beef from the pan, partially re-cover, and simmer for 1 hour more.

3 Remove the pan from the heat and let cool. Strain the stock into a bowl, cover with plastic wrap, and chill in the refrigerator for at least 1 hour and preferably overnight.

4 Remove and discard the layer of fat that has set on the surface. Use immediately or freeze for up to 6 months.

Chicken Stock

Makes 4$\frac{1}{2}$ pints

Ingredients

3 lb/1.3 kg chicken wings and necks
2 onions, cut into wedges
7 pints water
2 carrots, coarsely chopped
2 celery stalks, coarsely chopped
10 fresh parsley sprigs
4 fresh thyme sprigs
2 bay leaves
10 black peppercorns

1 Place the chicken and onions in a large, heavy pan and cook over low heat, stirring frequently, until browned all over.

2 Pour in the water and stir well, scraping up any sediment from the base of the pan. Bring to a boil and skim off the foam that rises to the surface.

3 Add the carrots, celery, parsley, thyme, bay leaves, and peppercorns, partially cover the pan, and simmer gently, stirring occasionally, for 3 hours.

4 Remove the pan from the heat and let cool. Strain the stock into a bowl, cover with plastic wrap, and chill in the refrigerator for at least 1 hour and preferably overnight.

5 Remove and discard the layer of fat that has set on the surface. Use immediately or freeze for up to 6 months.

Fish Stock

Makes 5²/₃ cups

Ingredients
1 lb 7 oz/650 g white fish heads, bones, and trimmings
1 onion, sliced
2 celery stalks, chopped
1 carrot, sliced
1 bay leaf
4 fresh parsley sprigs
4 black peppercorns
¹/₂ lemon, sliced
¹/₂ cup dry white wine
5²/₃ cups water

1 Cut out and discard the gills from the fish heads, then rinse the heads, bones, and trimmings. Place them in a large pan.

2 Add the remaining ingredients. Bring to a boil and skim off the foam that rises to the surface. Lower the heat, cover, and simmer for 25 minutes.

3 Remove the pan from the heat and let cool. Strain the stock into a bowl, without pressing down on the contents of the strainer. Use immediately or freeze for up to 3 months.

Vegetable Stock

Makes 8³/₄ cups

Ingredients
2 tbsp sunflower or corn oil
4 oz/115 g onions, finely chopped
4 oz/115 g leeks, finely chopped
4 oz/115 g carrots, finely chopped
4 celery stalks, finely chopped
3 oz/85 g fennel, finely chopped
3 oz/85 g tomatoes, finely chopped
4 pints water
1 bouquet garni

1 Heat the oil in a large, heavy pan. Add the onions and leeks and cook over low heat, stirring occasionally, for 5 minutes, until softened.

2 Add the carrots, celery, fennel, and tomatoes, cover, and cook, stirring occasionally, for 10 minutes. Pour in the water, add the bouquet garni, and bring to a boil. Lower the heat and simmer for 20 minutes.

3 Remove the pan from the heat and let cool. Strain the stock into a bowl. Use immediately or freeze for up to 3 months.

CHUNKY VEGETABLE SOUP

Put the carrots, onion, garlic, potatoes, celery, mushrooms, tomatoes, and stock into a large pan. Stir in the bay leaf and herbs. Bring to a boil, then reduce the heat, cover, and let simmer for 25 minutes.

Add the corn and cabbage and return to a boil. Reduce the heat, cover, and simmer for 5 minutes, or until the vegetables are tender. Remove and discard the bay leaf.

Season to taste with pepper.

Ladle into warmed bowls and serve at once with crusty bread rolls.

SERVES 6

2 carrots, sliced

1 onion, diced

1 garlic clove, crushed

12 oz/350 g new potatoes, diced

2 celery stalks, sliced

4 oz/115 g button mushrooms, quartered

14 oz/400 g canned chopped tomatoes in tomato juice

2½ cups vegetable stock

1 bay leaf

1 tsp dried mixed herbs or 1 tbsp chopped fresh mixed herbs

½ cup corn kernels, frozen or canned, drained

2 oz/55 g green cabbage, shredded

pepper

crusty whole wheat or white bread rolls, to serve

MINESTRONE

Heat the oil in a large pan. Add the garlic, onions, and prosciutto and cook over medium heat, stirring, for 3 minutes, until slightly softened. Add the red and orange bell peppers and the chopped tomatoes and cook for another 2 minutes, stirring. Stir in the stock, then add the celery, beans, cabbage, peas, and parsley. Season with salt and pepper. Bring to a boil, then lower the heat and simmer for 30 minutes.

Add the vermicelli to the pan. Cook for another 10–12 minutes, or according to the instructions on the package. Remove from the heat and ladle into serving bowls. Garnish with freshly grated Parmesan and serve with fresh crusty bread.

SERVES 4

2 tbsp olive oil

2 garlic cloves, chopped

2 red onions, chopped

2¾ oz/75 g prosciutto, sliced

1 red bell pepper, seeded and chopped

1 orange bell pepper, seeded and chopped

14 oz/400 g canned chopped tomatoes

4 cups vegetable stock

1 celery stalk, trimmed and sliced

14 oz/400 g canned borlotti beans, drained

3½ oz/100 g green leafy cabbage, shredded

2¾ oz/75 g frozen peas, thawed

1 tbsp chopped fresh parsley

2¾ oz/75 g dried vermicelli

salt and pepper

freshly grated Parmesan cheese, to garnish

fresh crusty bread, to serve

FRENCH ONION SOUP

SERVES 6

3 tbsp olive oil

1 lb 8 oz/675 g onions, thinly sliced

4 garlic cloves, 3 chopped and 1 peeled but kept whole

1 tsp sugar

2 tsp chopped fresh thyme

2 tbsp all-purpose flour

½ cup dry white wine

8 cups vegetable stock

6 slices of French bread

3 cups grated Swiss cheese

fresh thyme sprigs, to garnish

Heat the olive oil in a large, heavy-bottom pan, then add the onions and cook, stirring occasionally, for 10 minutes, until they are just beginning to brown. Stir in the chopped garlic, sugar, and thyme, then reduce the heat and cook, stirring occasionally, for 30 minutes, or until the onions are golden brown.

Sprinkle in the flour and cook, stirring, for 1–2 minutes. Stir in the wine. Gradually stir in the stock and bring to a boil, skimming off any foam that rises to the surface, then reduce the heat and simmer for 45 minutes. Meanwhile, toast the bread on both sides under a preheated medium broiler. Rub the toast with the whole garlic clove.

Ladle the soup into 6 flameproof bowls set on a baking sheet. Float a piece of toast in each bowl and divide the grated cheese among them. Place under a preheated medium–hot broiler for 2–3 minutes, or until the cheese has just melted. Garnish with thyme sprigs and serve.

ROASTED VEGETABLE SOUP

Preheat the oven to 375°F/190°C.

Brush a large, shallow baking pan with some of the olive oil. Laying them cut-side down, arrange the tomatoes, bell peppers, zucchini, and eggplant in one layer (use two dishes, if necessary). Tuck the garlic cloves and onion pieces into the gaps and drizzle the vegetables with the remaining olive oil. Season lightly with salt and pepper and sprinkle with the thyme.

Place in the preheated oven and bake, uncovered, for 30–35 minutes, or until soft and browned around the edges. Cool, then scrape out the eggplant flesh and remove the skin from the bell peppers.

Working in batches, put the eggplant and bell pepper flesh, together with the tomatoes, zucchini, garlic, and onions, into a food processor and chop to the consistency of salsa; do not purée. Alternatively, place in a bowl and chop together with a knife.

Combine the stock and chopped vegetable mixture in a saucepan and simmer over medium heat for 20–30 minutes, until all the vegetables are tender and the flavors have completely blended.

Stir in the cream and simmer over low heat for about 5 minutes, stirring occasionally, until hot. Taste and adjust the seasoning, if necessary. Ladle the soup into warmed bowls, garnish with basil, and serve.

SERVES 6

3 tbsp olive oil

1 lb 9 oz/700 g ripe tomatoes, skinned, cored, and halved

3 large yellow bell peppers, seeded and halved

3 zucchini, halved lengthwise

1 small eggplant, halved lengthwise

4 garlic cloves, halved

2 onions, cut into eighths

pinch of dried thyme

4 cups chicken, vegetable, or beef stock

½ cup light cream

salt and pepper

shredded basil leaves, to garnish

SQUASH, SWEET POTATO & GARLIC SOUP

Preheat the oven to 375°F/190°C.

Cut the sweet potato, squash, and shallots in half lengthwise, through to the stem end. Scoop the seeds out of the squash. Brush the cut sides with the oil.

Put the vegetables, cut-side down, in a shallow roasting pan. Add the garlic cloves. Roast in the preheated oven for about 40 minutes, until tender and light brown. Set aside to cool.

When cool, scoop the flesh from the potato and squash halves, and put in a saucepan. Remove the peel from the garlic and shallots and add the soft insides to the other vegetables.

Add the stock and a pinch of salt. Bring just to a boil, reduce the heat, and simmer, partially covered, for about 30 minutes, stirring occasionally, until the vegetables are very tender.

Cool the soup slightly, and then transfer to a food processor or blender and process until smooth, working in batches, if necessary. (If using a food processor, strain off the cooking liquid and reserve. Process the soup solids with enough cooking liquid to moisten them, then combine with the remaining liquid.)

Return the soup to the rinsed-out pan and stir in the cream. Season to taste with salt and pepper, then simmer for 5–10 minutes until completely heated through. Ladle into warmed serving bowls, garnish with pepper and snipped chives, and serve.

SERVES 6–8

1 sweet potato, about 12 oz/350 g

1 acorn squash

4 shallots

2 tbsp olive oil

5–6 garlic cloves, unpeeled

3¾ cups chicken stock

½ cup light cream

salt and pepper

snipped chives, to garnish

VICHYSSOISE

SERVES 6

3 large leeks

3 tbsp butter

1 onion, thinly sliced

1 lb/450 g potatoes, chopped

3½ cups vegetable stock

2 tsp lemon juice

pinch of ground nutmeg

¼ tsp ground coriander

1 bay leaf

1 egg yolk

⅔ cup light cream

salt and pepper

freshly snipped chives, to garnish

Trim the leeks, removing most of the green parts. Slice the white parts of the leeks very finely.

Melt the butter in a saucepan. Add the leeks and onion and cook, stirring occasionally, for about 5 minutes without browning.

Add the potatoes, stock, lemon juice, nutmeg, coriander, and bay leaf to the pan, season to taste with salt and pepper, and bring to a boil. Cover and simmer for about 30 minutes, until all the vegetables are very soft.

Cool the soup a little, remove and discard the bay leaf, and then press through a strainer or process in a food processor or blender until smooth. Pour into a clean pan.

Blend the egg yolk into the cream, add a little of the soup to the mixture, and then whisk it all back into the soup and reheat gently, without boiling. Adjust the seasoning to taste. Cool, transfer to a bowl, cover with plastic wrap, and then chill thoroughly in the refrigerator.

Serve the soup sprinkled with freshly snipped chives.

BEEF GOULASH SOUP

Heat the oil in a large, wide saucepan over medium–high heat. Add the beef and sprinkle with salt and pepper. Cook until lightly browned.

Reduce the heat and add the onions and garlic. Cook for about 3 minutes, stirring frequently, until the onions are softened. Stir in the flour and continue cooking for 1 minute.

Gradually stir in the water and combine well, scraping the bottom of the pan to mix in the flour. Stir in the tomatoes, carrot, pepper, paprika, caraway seeds, oregano, and stock.

Bring just to a boil. Reduce the heat, cover, and simmer gently for about 40 minutes, stirring occasionally, until all the vegetables are tender.

Add the tagliatelle to the soup and simmer for an additional 20 minutes, or until the tagliatelle is cooked.

Taste the soup and adjust the seasoning, if necessary. Ladle into warmed bowls and top each with a tablespoonful of sour cream. Garnish with cilantro and serve.

SERVES 6

- 1 tbsp olive oil
- 1 lb 2 oz/500 g fresh lean ground beef
- 2 onions, finely chopped
- 2 garlic cloves, finely chopped
- 2 tbsp all-purpose flour
- 1 cup water
- 14 oz/400 g canned chopped tomatoes
- 1 carrot, finely chopped
- 8 oz/225 g red bell pepper, roasted, peeled, seeded, and chopped
- 1 tsp Hungarian paprika
- ¼ tsp caraway seeds
- pinch of dried oregano
- 4 cups beef stock
- 2 oz/55 g tagliatelle, broken into small pieces
- salt and pepper
- sour cream and sprigs of fresh cilantro, to garnish

BEEF &
BEAN SOUP

Heat the oil in a large pan over medium heat. Add the onion and garlic and cook, stirring frequently, for 3 minutes, or until softened. Add the bell pepper and carrots and cook for an additional 5 minutes.

Meanwhile, drain the peas, reserving the liquid from the can. Place two thirds of the peas, reserving the remainder, in a food processor or blender with the pea liquid and process until smooth.

Add the ground beef to the pan and cook, stirring constantly to break up any lumps, until well browned. Add the spices and cook, stirring, for 2 minutes. Add the cabbage, tomatoes, stock, and processed peas and season to taste with salt and pepper. Bring to a boil, then reduce the heat, cover, and simmer for 15 minutes, or until the vegetables are tender.

Stir in the reserved peas, cover, and simmer for an additional 5 minutes. Ladle the soup into warmed soup bowls and serve.

SERVES 4

2 tbsp vegetable oil

1 large onion, finely chopped

2 garlic cloves, finely chopped

1 green bell pepper, seeded and sliced

2 carrots, sliced

14 oz/400 g canned black-eyed peas

1 cup ground fresh beef

1 tsp each ground cumin, chili powder, and paprika

¼ head of cabbage, sliced

8 oz/225 g tomatoes, peeled and chopped

2½ cups beef stock

salt and pepper

CHORIZO & RED KIDNEY BEAN SOUP

SERVES 4

2 tbsp olive oil

2 garlic cloves, chopped

2 red onions, chopped

1 red bell pepper, seeded and chopped

2 tbsp cornstarch

4 cups vegetable stock

1 lb/450 g potatoes, peeled, halved, and sliced

5½ oz/150 g chorizo, sliced

2 zucchini, trimmed and sliced

7 oz/200 g canned red kidney beans, drained

½ cup heavy cream

salt and pepper

slices of fresh crusty bread, to serve

Heat the oil in a large pan. Add the garlic and onions and cook over medium heat, stirring, for 3 minutes, until slightly softened. Add the bell pepper and cook for another 3 minutes, stirring. In a bowl, mix the cornstarch with enough stock to make a smooth paste and stir it into the pan. Cook, stirring, for 2 minutes. Stir in the remaining stock, then add the potatoes and season with salt and pepper. Bring to a boil, then lower the heat and simmer for 25 minutes, until the vegetables are tender.

Add the chorizo, zucchini, and kidney beans to the pan. Cook for 10 minutes, then stir in the cream and cook for another 5 minutes. Remove from the heat and ladle into serving bowls. Serve with slices of fresh crusty bread.

BACON & LENTIL SOUP

Heat a large, heavy-bottom saucepan or flameproof casserole. Add the bacon and cook over medium heat, stirring, for 4–5 minutes, or until the fat runs. Add the chopped onion, carrots, celery, turnip, and potato and cook, stirring frequently, for 5 minutes.

Add the lentils and bouquet garni and pour in the stock. Bring to a boil, reduce the heat, and simmer for 1 hour, or until the lentils are tender.

Remove and discard the bouquet garni and season the soup to taste with pepper, and with salt if necessary. Ladle into warmed soup bowls and serve.

SERVES 4

1 lb/450 g thick, rindless smoked bacon strips, diced

1 onion, chopped

2 carrots, sliced

2 celery stalks, chopped

1 turnip, chopped

1 large potato, chopped

generous 2¼ cups Puy lentils

1 bouquet garni

4 cups chicken stock

salt and pepper

CHEESE & BACON SOUP

Melt the butter in a large pan over medium heat. Add the garlic and onion and cook, stirring, for 3 minutes, until slightly softened. Add the chopped bacon and leeks and cook for another 3 minutes, stirring.

In a bowl, mix the flour with enough stock to make a smooth paste and stir it into the pan. Cook, stirring, for 2 minutes. Pour in the remaining stock, then add the potatoes. Season with salt and pepper. Bring the soup to a boil, then lower the heat and simmer gently for 25 minutes, until the potatoes are tender and cooked through.

Stir in the cream and cook for 5 minutes, then gradually stir in the cheese until melted. Remove from the heat and ladle into individual serving bowls. Garnish with grated cheddar cheese and serve immediately.

SERVES 4

2 tbsp butter

2 garlic cloves, chopped

1 large onion, sliced

9 oz/250 g smoked lean bacon, chopped

2 large leeks, trimmed and sliced

2 tbsp all-purpose flour

4 cups vegetable stock

1 lb/450 g potatoes, chopped

scant ½ cup heavy cream

3 cups grated cheddar cheese, plus extra to garnish

salt and pepper

WONTON SOUP

SERVES 6–8

8 cups chicken stock

2 tsp salt

½ tsp white pepper

2 tbsp finely chopped scallion,
  to serve

1 tbsp chopped cilantro leaves,
  to serve

wontons

6 oz/175 g ground pork,
  not too lean

8 oz/225 g raw shrimp, peeled,
  deveined, and chopped

½ tsp finely chopped fresh ginger

1 tbsp light soy sauce

1 tbsp Chinese rice wine

2 tsp finely chopped scallion

pinch of sugar

pinch of white pepper

dash of sesame oil

30 square wonton wrappers

1 egg white, lightly beaten

For the wonton filling, mix together the pork, shrimp, ginger, soy sauce, rice wine, scallion, sugar, pepper, and sesame oil, and stir well until the texture is thick and pasty. Set aside for at least 20 minutes.

To make the wontons, place a teaspoon of the filling at the center of a wrapper. Brush the edges with a little egg white. Bring the opposite points toward each other and press the edges together, creating a flowerlike shape. Repeat with the remaining wrappers and filling.

To make the soup, bring the stock to a boil and add the salt and pepper. Boil the wontons in the stock for about 5 minutes, or until the wrappers begin to wrinkle around the filling.

To serve, divide the scallion among individual bowls, then spoon in the wontons and soup, and sprinkle with the cilantro.

SAUSAGE & RED CABBAGE SOUP

Heat the oil in a large pan. Add the garlic and onion and cook over medium heat, stirring, for 3 minutes, until slightly softened. Add the leek and cook for another 3 minutes, stirring.

In a bowl, mix the cornstarch with enough stock to make a smooth paste, then stir it into the pan. Cook, stirring, for 2 minutes. Stir in the remaining stock, then add the potatoes and sausages. Season with salt and pepper. Bring to a boil, then lower the heat and simmer for 25 minutes.

Add the red cabbage and black-eyed peas and cook for 10 minutes, then stir in the cream and cook for another 5 minutes. Remove from the heat and ladle into serving bowls. Garnish with ground paprika and serve immediately.

SERVES 4

2 tbsp olive oil

1 garlic clove, chopped

1 large onion, chopped

1 large leek, sliced

2 tbsp cornstarch

4 cups vegetable stock

1 lb/450 g potatoes, sliced

7 oz/200 g skinless sausages, sliced

5½ oz/150 g red cabbage, chopped

7 oz/200 g canned black-eyed peas, drained

½ cup heavy cream

salt and pepper

ground paprika, to garnish

ASIAN
LAMB SOUP

Trim all visible fat from the lamb and slice the meat thinly. Cut the slices into bite-size pieces. Spread the meat in one layer on a plate and sprinkle over the garlic and 1 tablespoon of the soy sauce. Marinate, covered, for at least 10 minutes or up to 1 hour.

Put the stock in a saucepan with the ginger, lemongrass, remaining soy sauce, and the chili paste. Bring just to a boil, reduce the heat, cover, and simmer for 10–15 minutes.

When ready to serve the soup, drop the tomatoes, scallions, bean sprouts, and cilantro leaves into the stock.

Heat the oil in a skillet and add the lamb with its marinade. Stir-fry the lamb just until it is no longer red and divide among the warmed bowls.

Ladle over the hot stock and serve immediately.

SERVES 4

5½ oz/150 g lean tender lamb, such as neck fillet or leg steak

2 garlic cloves, very finely chopped

2 tbsp soy sauce

5 cups chicken stock

1 tbsp grated fresh ginger

2-inch/5-cm piece lemongrass, sliced into very thin rounds

¼ tsp chili paste, or to taste

6–8 cherry tomatoes, quartered

4 scallions, finely sliced

1¾ oz/50 g bean sprouts, snapped in half

2 tbsp cilantro leaves

1 tsp olive oil

CREAM OF CHICKEN SOUP

SERVES 4

3 tbsp butter

4 shallots, chopped

1 leek, sliced

1 lb/450 g skinless chicken
  breasts, chopped

2½ cups chicken stock

1 tbsp chopped fresh parsley

1 tbsp chopped fresh thyme,
  plus extra sprigs to garnish

¾ cup heavy cream

salt and pepper

Melt the butter in a large pan over medium heat. Add the shallots
and cook, stirring, for 3 minutes, until slightly softened. Add the
leek and cook for another 5 minutes, stirring. Add the chicken,
stock, and herbs, and season with salt and pepper. Bring to a
boil, then lower the heat and simmer for 25 minutes, until the
chicken is tender and cooked through. Remove from the heat
and cool for 10 minutes.

Transfer the soup into a food processor or blender and process
until smooth (you may need to do this in batches). Return the
soup to the rinsed-out pan and warm over low heat for 5 minutes.

Stir in the cream and cook for another 2 minutes, then remove
from the heat and ladle into serving bowls. Garnish with sprigs of
thyme and serve immediately.

soups

45

CHICKEN-NOODLE SOUP

Put the chicken breasts and water in a pan over high heat and bring to a boil. Lower the heat to its lowest setting and simmer, skimming the surface until no more foam rises. Add the onion, garlic, ginger, peppercorns, cloves, star anise, and a pinch of salt, and continue to simmer for 20 minutes, or until the chicken is tender and cooked through. Meanwhile, grate the carrot along its length on the coarse side of a grater so you get long, thin strips.

Strain the chicken, reserving about 5 cups of stock but discarding any flavoring solids. (At this point you can let the stock cool and refrigerate overnight, so any fat solidifies and can be lifted off and discarded.) Return the stock to the rinsed-out pan with the carrot, celery, baby corn, and scallions, and bring to a boil. Boil until the baby corn are almost tender, then add the noodles and continue boiling for 2 minutes.

Meanwhile, chop the chicken, and add to the pan and continue cooking for about 1 minute longer until the chicken is reheated and the noodles are soft. Add seasoning to taste.

SERVES 4–6

2 skinless chicken breasts

8 cups water

1 onion, unpeeled, cut in half

1 large garlic clove, cut in half

½-inch/1-cm piece fresh ginger, peeled and sliced

4 black peppercorns, lightly crushed

4 cloves

2 star anise

1 carrot, peeled

1 celery stalk, chopped

3½ oz/100 g baby corn, cut in half lengthwise and chopped

2 scallions, finely shredded

4 oz/115 g dried rice vermicelli noodles

salt and pepper

CHICKEN & LEEK SOUP

Heat the oil in a large pan over medium heat, add the onions, carrots, and the 2 coarsely chopped leeks, and cook for 3–4 minutes until just golden brown.

Wipe the chicken inside and out and remove and discard any excess skin and fat.

Put the chicken into the pan with the cooked vegetables and add the bay leaves. Pour in enough cold water just to cover and season well with salt and pepper. Bring to a boil, then reduce the heat, cover, and simmer for 1–1½ hours. Skim off any foam that forms from time to time.

Remove the chicken from the stock, remove and discard the skin, then remove all the meat. Cut the meat into neat pieces.

Strain the stock through a colander, discard the vegetables and bay leaves, and return to the rinsed-out pan. Expect to have 4–5 cups of stock. If you have time, it is a good idea to let the stock cool so that the fat solidifies and can be removed. If not, blot the fat off the surface with paper towels.

Heat the stock to simmering point, add the sliced leeks and prunes to the pan, and heat for about 1 minute. Return the chicken to the pan and heat through. Serve immediately in warmed deep dishes, garnished with the parsley.

SERVES 6–8

2 tbsp olive oil

2 onions, coarsely chopped

2 carrots, coarsely chopped

5 leeks, 2 coarsely chopped, 3 thinly sliced

1 chicken, weighing 3 lb/1.3 kg

2 bay leaves

6 prunes, pitted and sliced

salt and pepper

sprigs of fresh parsley, to garnish

CHICKEN & POTATO SOUP WITH BACON

SERVES 4

1 tbsp butter

2 garlic cloves, chopped

1 onion, sliced

9 oz/250 g smoked lean bacon, chopped

2 large leeks, sliced

2 tbsp all-purpose flour

4 cups chicken stock

1 lb 12 oz/800 g potatoes, chopped

7 oz/200 g skinless chicken breast, chopped

4 tbsp heavy cream

salt and pepper

cooked bacon and sprigs of fresh flat-leaf parsley, to garnish

Melt the butter in a large pan over medium heat. Add the garlic and onion and cook, stirring, for 3 minutes, until slightly softened. Add the chopped bacon and leeks and cook for another 3 minutes, stirring.

In a bowl, mix the flour with enough stock to make a smooth paste and stir it into the pan. Cook, stirring, for 2 minutes. Pour in the remaining stock, then add the potatoes and chicken. Season with salt and pepper. Bring to a boil, then lower the heat and simmer for 25 minutes, until the chicken and potatoes are tender and cooked through.

Stir in the cream and cook for another 2 minutes, then remove from the heat and ladle into serving bowls. Garnish with the cooked bacon and flat-leaf parsley and serve immediately.

CHICKEN GUMBO SOUP

Heat the oil in a large, heavy-bottom saucepan over medium–low heat and stir in the flour. Cook for about 15 minutes, stirring occasionally, until the mixture is a rich golden brown.

Add the onion, green bell pepper, and celery and continue cooking for about 10 minutes until the onion softens.

Slowly pour in the stock and bring to a boil, stirring well and scraping the bottom of the pan to mix in the flour. Remove the pan from the heat.

Add the tomatoes and garlic. Stir in the okra and rice and season to taste with salt and pepper. Reduce the heat, cover, and simmer for 20 minutes, or until the okra is tender.

Add the chicken and sausage and continue simmering for about 10 minutes. Taste and adjust the seasoning, if necessary, and ladle into warmed bowls to serve.

SERVES 6

2 tbsp olive oil

4 tbsp all-purpose flour

1 onion, finely chopped

1 small green bell pepper, seeded and finely chopped

1 celery stalk, finely chopped

5 cups chicken stock

14 oz/400 g canned chopped tomatoes

3 garlic cloves, finely chopped or crushed

4½ oz/125 g okra, stems removed, cut into ¼-inch/5-mm thick slices

4 tbsp white rice

7 oz/200 g cooked chicken, cubed

4 oz/115 g cooked garlic sausage, sliced or cubed

salt and pepper

THAI CHICKEN-COCONUT SOUP

Put the dried noodles in a large bowl with enough lukewarm water to cover and soak for 20 minutes, until soft. Alternatively, cook according to the package instructions. Drain well and set aside.

Meanwhile, bring the stock to a boil in a large pan over high heat. Lower the heat, add the lemongrass, ginger, lime leaves, and chile, and simmer for 5 minutes. Add the chicken and continue simmering for an additional 3 minutes, or until cooked. Stir in the coconut cream, nam pla, and lime juice, and continue simmering for 3 minutes. Add the bean sprouts and scallions and simmer for an additional 1 minute. Taste and gradually add extra nam pla or lime juice at this point, if needed. Remove and discard the lemongrass stalk.

Divide the noodles among 4 bowls. Bring the soup back to a boil, then ladle into the bowls. The heat of the soup will warm the noodles. To garnish, sprinkle with cilantro leaves.

SERVES 4

4 oz/115 g dried cellophane noodles

5 cups chicken stock or vegetable stock

1 lemongrass stalk, crushed

½-inch/1-cm piece fresh ginger, peeled and very finely chopped

2 fresh kaffir lime leaves, thinly sliced

1 fresh red chile, or to taste, seeded and thinly sliced

2 skinless, boneless chicken breasts, thinly sliced

scant 1 cup coconut cream

about 2 tbsp nam pla (Thai fish sauce)

about 1 tbsp fresh lime juice

scant ½ cup bean sprouts

4 scallions, green parts only, finely sliced

fresh cilantro leaves, to garnish

TURKEY & LENTIL SOUP

SERVES 4

1 tbsp olive oil

1 garlic clove, chopped

1 large onion, chopped

7 oz/200 g white mushrooms, sliced

1 red bell pepper, seeded and chopped

6 tomatoes, skinned, seeded, and chopped

4 cups chicken stock

²/₃ cup red wine

3 oz/85 g cauliflower florets

1 carrot, chopped

1 cup red lentils

12 oz/350 g cooked turkey, chopped

1 zucchini, chopped

1 tbsp shredded fresh basil

salt and pepper

sprigs of fresh basil, to garnish

Heat the oil in a large pan. Add the garlic and onion and cook over medium heat, stirring, for 3 minutes, until slightly softened. Add the mushrooms, bell pepper, and tomatoes, and cook for another 5 minutes, stirring. Pour in the stock and red wine, then add the cauliflower, carrot, and red lentils. Season to taste with salt and pepper. Bring to a boil, then lower the heat and simmer for 25 minutes, until the vegetables are tender and cooked through.

Add the turkey and zucchini to the pan and cook for 10 minutes. Stir in the shredded basil and cook for another 5 minutes, then remove from the heat and ladle into serving bowls. Garnish with fresh basil sprigs and serve immediately.

DUCK WITH SCALLION SOUP

Slash the skin of the duck 3 or 4 times with a sharp knife and rub in the curry paste. Cook the duck breasts, skin-side down, in a wok or skillet over high heat for 2–3 minutes. Turn over, reduce the heat, and cook for an additional 3–4 minutes, until cooked through. Lift out and slice thickly. Set aside and keep warm.

Meanwhile, heat the oil in a wok or large skillet and stir-fry half the scallions with the garlic, ginger, carrots, and red bell pepper for 2–3 minutes. Pour in the stock and add the chili sauce, soy sauce, and mushrooms. Bring to a boil, reduce the heat, and simmer for 4–5 minutes.

Ladle the soup into warmed bowls, top with the duck slices, and garnish with the remaining scallions. Serve immediately.

SERVES 4

2 duck breasts, skin on

2 tbsp red curry paste

2 tbsp vegetable oil or peanut oil

bunch of scallions, chopped

2 garlic cloves, crushed

2-inch/5-cm piece fresh ginger, grated

2 carrots, thinly sliced

1 red bell pepper, seeded and cut into strips

4 cups chicken stock

2 tbsp sweet chili sauce

3–4 tbsp Thai soy sauce

14 oz/400 g canned straw mushrooms, drained

SEAFOOD CHOWDER

Discard any mussels with broken shells or any that refuse to close when tapped. Rinse and pull off any beards. Put the mussels in a large heavy-bottom saucepan. Cover tightly and cook over high heat for about 4 minutes, or until the mussels open, shaking the pan occasionally. Discard any that remain closed. When they are cool enough to handle, remove the mussels from the shells and set aside.

Put the flour in a mixing bowl and very slowly whisk in enough of the stock to make a thick paste. Whisk in a little more stock to make a smooth liquid.

Melt the butter in a heavy-bottom saucepan over medium–low heat. Add the onion, cover, and cook for 3 minutes, stirring frequently, until it softens.

Add the remaining fish stock and bring to a boil. Slowly whisk in the flour mixture until well combined and bring back to a boil, whisking constantly. Add the mussel cooking liquid. Season with salt, if needed, and pepper. Reduce the heat and simmer, partially covered, for 15 minutes.

Add the whitefish and the mussels and continue simmering, stirring occasionally, for about 5 minutes, or until the fish is cooked and begins to flake.

Stir in the shrimp and cream. Taste and adjust the seasoning. Simmer for 2–3 minutes longer to heat through. Ladle into warmed bowls, sprinkle with dill, and serve.

SERVES 6

2 lb 4 oz/1 kg live mussels

4 tbsp all-purpose flour

6¼ cups fish stock

1 tbsp butter

1 large onion, finely chopped

12 oz/350 g skinless whitefish fillets, such as cod, sole, or haddock

7 oz/200 g cooked or raw peeled shrimp

1¼ cups heavy cream

salt and pepper

snipped fresh dill, to garnish

BOUILLABAISSE

SERVES 4

scant ½ cup olive oil

3 garlic cloves, chopped

2 onions, chopped

2 tomatoes, seeded and chopped

2¾ cups fish stock

1¾ cups white wine

1 bay leaf

pinch of saffron threads

2 tbsp chopped fresh basil

2 tbsp chopped fresh parsley

7 oz/200 g live mussels

9 oz/250 g snapper or monkfish fillets

9 oz/250 g haddock fillets, skinned

7 oz/200 g shrimp, peeled and deveined

3½ oz/100 g scallops

salt and pepper

Heat the oil in a large pan over medium heat. Add the garlic and onions and cook, stirring, for 3 minutes. Stir in the tomatoes, stock, wine, bay leaf, saffron, and herbs. Bring to a boil, reduce the heat, cover, and simmer for 30 minutes.

Meanwhile, soak the mussels in lightly salted water for 10 minutes. Scrub the shells under cold running water and pull off any beards. Discard any mussels with broken shells or any that refuse to close when tapped. Put the rest into a large pan with a little water, bring to a boil, and cook over high heat for 4 minutes. Remove from the heat and discard any that remain closed.

When the tomato mixture is cooked, rinse the fish fillets, pat dry, and cut into chunks. Add to the pan and simmer for 5 minutes. Add the mussels, shrimp, and scallops, and season with salt and pepper to taste. Cook for 3 minutes, until the fish is cooked through. Remove from the heat, discard the bay leaf, and ladle into serving bowls.

SALMON & LEEK SOUP

Heat the oil in a large, heavy-bottom saucepan over medium heat. Add the onion and leeks and cook for about 3 minutes until they begin to soften.

Add the potato, stock, water, and bay leaf with a large pinch of salt. Bring to a boil, reduce the heat, cover, and cook gently for about 25 minutes until the vegetables are tender. Remove the bay leaf.

Let the soup cool slightly, then transfer about half of it to a food processor or blender and process until smooth. (If using a food processor, strain off the cooking liquid and reserve. Purée half the soup solids with enough cooking liquid to moisten them, then combine with the remaining liquid.)

Return the processed soup to the saucepan and stir to blend. Reheat gently over medium–low heat.

Season the salmon with salt and pepper and add to the soup. Continue cooking for about 5 minutes, stirring occasionally, until the fish is tender and starts to break up. Stir in the cream, taste, and adjust the seasoning, adding a little lemon juice if desired. Ladle into warmed bowls, garnish with chervil or parsley, and serve.

SERVES 4

1 tbsp olive oil

1 large onion, finely chopped

3 large leeks, including green parts, thinly sliced

1 potato, finely diced

2 cups fish stock

3 cups water

1 bay leaf

10½ oz/300 g skinless salmon fillet, cut into ½-inch/1-cm cubes

⅓ cup heavy cream

fresh lemon juice (optional)

salt and pepper

sprigs of fresh chervil or parsley, to garnish

THAI-STYLE SEAFOOD SOUP

Put the stock in a saucepan with the lemongrass, lime rind, ginger, and chili paste. Bring just to a boil, reduce the heat, cover, and simmer for 10–15 minutes.

Cut the shrimp almost in half lengthwise, keeping the tails intact.

Strain the stock, return to the saucepan, and bring to a simmer. Add the scallions and cook for 2–3 minutes. Taste and season with salt, if needed, and stir in a little more chili paste if desired.

Add the scallops and shrimp and poach for about 1 minute until they turn opaque and the shrimp curl.

Stir in the fresh cilantro leaves, ladle the soup into warmed bowls, dividing the shellfish evenly, and garnish with chiles.

SERVES 4

5 cups fish stock

1 lemongrass stalk, split lengthwise

pared rind of ½ lime, or 1 lime leaf

1-inch/2.5-cm piece fresh ginger, sliced

¼ tsp chili paste, or to taste

7 oz/200 g large or medium raw shrimp, peeled

4–6 scallions, sliced

9 oz/250 g scallops

2 tbsp fresh cilantro leaves

salt

finely sliced red chiles, to garnish

GENOESE
FISH SOUP

SERVES 6

2 tbsp butter

1 onion, chopped

1 garlic clove, finely chopped

2 oz/55 g rindless bacon, diced

2 celery stalks, chopped

14 oz/400 g canned chopped
   tomatoes

²/₃ cup dry white wine

1¼ cups fish stock

4 fresh basil leaves, torn

2 tbsp chopped fresh flat-leaf
   parsley

1 lb/450 g whitefish fillets, such
   as cod or monkfish, skinned and
   chopped

4 oz/115 g cooked peeled shrimp

salt and pepper

Melt the butter in a large, heavy-bottom saucepan. Add the
onion and garlic and cook over low heat, stirring occasionally,
for 5 minutes, or until softened.

Add the bacon and celery and cook, stirring frequently, for an
additional 2 minutes.

Add the tomatoes, wine, stock, basil, and 1 tablespoon of the
parsley. Season to taste with salt and pepper. Bring to a boil,
then reduce the heat and simmer for 10 minutes.

Add the whitefish and cook for 5 minutes, or until it is opaque.
Add the shrimp and heat through gently for 3 minutes. Ladle
into warmed serving bowls, garnish with the remaining chopped
parsley, and serve immediately.

CORN & CRAB SOUP

Heat the oil in a large skillet and sauté the garlic, shallots, lemongrass, and ginger over low heat, stirring occasionally, for 2–3 minutes, until softened. Add the stock and coconut milk and bring to a boil. Add the corn, reduce the heat, and simmer gently for 3–4 minutes.

Add the crabmeat, fish sauce, lime juice, and sugar, and simmer gently for 1 minute. Ladle into warmed bowls, garnish with the chopped cilantro, and serve immediately.

SERVES 6

2 tbsp vegetable oil or peanut oil

4 garlic cloves, finely chopped

5 shallots, finely chopped

2 lemongrass stalks, finely chopped

1-inch/2.5-cm piece fresh ginger, finely chopped

4 cups chicken stock

14 oz/400 g canned coconut milk

1½ cups frozen corn kernels

12 oz/350 g canned crabmeat, drained and shredded

2 tbsp fish sauce

juice of 1 lime

1 tsp jaggery or light brown sugar

small bunch of fresh cilantro, chopped, to garnish

CLAM & CORN CHOWDER

Melt the butter in a large saucepan over medium–low heat. Add the onion and carrot and cook for 3–4 minutes, stirring frequently, until the onion is softened. Stir in the flour and continue cooking for 2 minutes.

Slowly add about half the stock and stir well, scraping the bottom of the pan to mix in the flour. Pour in the remaining stock and the water and bring just to a boil, stirring.

Add the potatoes, corn, and milk and stir to combine. Reduce the heat and simmer gently, partially covered, for about 20 minutes, stirring occasionally, until all the vegetables are tender.

Chop the clams, if large. Stir in the clams and continue cooking for about 5 minutes until heated through. Taste and adjust the seasoning, if needed.

Ladle the soup into bowls and sprinkle with parsley.

SERVES 4

4 tsp butter

1 large onion, finely chopped

1 small carrot, finely diced

3 tbsp all-purpose flour

1¼ cups fish stock

¾ cup water

1 lb/450 g potatoes, diced

1 cup cooked or defrosted frozen corn

2 cups whole milk

10 oz/280 g canned clams, drained and rinsed

salt and pepper

chopped fresh parsley, to garnish

MEAT

POT ROAST
WITH POTATOES
& DILL

Preheat the oven to 275°F/140°C. Mix 2 tablespoons of the flour with the salt and pepper in a shallow dish. Dip the meat to coat. Heat the oil in a flameproof casserole and brown the meat all over. Transfer to a plate. Add half the butter to the casserole and cook the onion, celery, carrots, dill seeds, and thyme for 5 minutes. Return the meat and juices to the casserole.

Pour in the wine and enough stock to reach one-third of the way up the meat. Bring to a boil, cover, and cook in the oven for 3 hours, turning the meat every 30 minutes. After it has been cooking for 2 hours, add the potatoes and more stock if necessary.

When ready, transfer the meat and vegetables to a warmed serving dish. Strain the cooking liquid to remove any solids, then return the liquid to the casserole.

Mix the remaining butter and flour to a paste. Bring the cooking liquid to a boil. Whisk in small pieces of the flour and butter paste, whisking constantly until the sauce is smooth. Pour the sauce over the meat and vegetables. Sprinkle with the fresh dill to serve.

SERVES 6

- 2½ tbsp all-purpose flour
- 1 tsp salt
- ¼ tsp pepper
- 1 rolled brisket of beef, weighing 3 lb 8 oz/1.6 kg
- 2 tbsp vegetable oil
- 2 tbsp butter
- 1 onion, finely chopped
- 2 celery stalks, diced
- 2 carrots, peeled and diced
- 1 tsp dill seeds
- 1 tsp dried thyme or oregano
- 1½ cups red wine
- ⅔–1 cup beef stock
- 4–5 potatoes, cut into large chunks and boiled until just tender
- 2 tbsp chopped fresh dill, to serve

BEEF
STROGANOFF

Place the dried porcini mushrooms in a bowl and cover with hot water. Let soak for 20 minutes. Meanwhile, cut the beef against the grain into ¼-inch/5-mm thick slices, then into ½-inch/1-cm long strips, and reserve.

Drain the mushrooms, reserving the soaking liquid, and chop. Strain the soaking liquid through a fine-mesh strainer or coffee filter and reserve.

Heat half the oil in a large skillet. Add the shallots and cook over low heat, stirring occasionally, for 5 minutes, or until softened. Add the dried mushrooms, reserved soaking water, and whole cremini mushrooms and cook, stirring frequently, for 10 minutes, or until almost all of the liquid has evaporated, then transfer the mixture to a plate.

Heat the remaining oil in the skillet, add the beef and cook, stirring frequently, for 4 minutes, or until browned all over. You may need to do this in batches. Return the mushroom mixture to the skillet and season to taste with salt and pepper. Place the mustard and cream in a small bowl and stir to mix, then fold into the mixture. Heat through gently, then serve with freshly cooked pasta, garnished with chives.

SERVES 4

½ oz/15 g dried porcini mushrooms

12 oz/350 g beef tenderloin

2 tbsp olive oil

4 oz/115 g shallots, sliced

6 oz/175 g cremini mushrooms

½ tsp Dijon mustard

5 tbsp heavy cream

salt and pepper

freshly cooked pasta, to serve

fresh chives, to garnish

CHILI CON CARNE

SERVES 4

1 lb 10 oz/750 g lean braising beef

2 tbsp vegetable oil

1 large onion, sliced

2–4 garlic cloves, crushed

1 tbsp all-purpose flour

generous 1¾ cups tomato juice

14 oz/400 g canned tomatoes

1–2 tbsp sweet chili sauce

1 tsp ground cumin

15 oz/425 g canned red kidney beans, drained and rinsed

½ tsp dried oregano

1–2 tbsp chopped fresh parsley

salt and pepper

sprigs of fresh herbs, to garnish

freshly cooked rice and tortillas, to serve

Preheat the oven to 325°F/160°C. Using a sharp knife, cut the beef into ¾-inch/2-cm cubes. Heat the vegetable oil in a large flameproof casserole and cook the beef over medium heat until well seared on all sides. Remove the beef from the casserole with a slotted spoon and set aside until ready to use.

Add the onion and garlic to the casserole and cook until lightly browned, then stir in the flour and cook for 1–2 minutes.

Stir in the tomato juice and tomatoes and bring to a boil. Return the beef to the casserole and add the chili sauce, cumin, and salt and pepper to taste. Cover and cook in the preheated oven for 1½ hours, or until the beef is almost tender.

Stir in the kidney beans, oregano, and parsley, and adjust the seasoning to taste, if necessary. Cover the casserole and return to the oven for 45 minutes. Transfer to 4 large, warmed serving plates, garnish with sprigs of fresh herbs, and serve immediately with freshly cooked rice and tortillas.

BEEF GOULASH

Heat the vegetable oil in a large pan and cook the onion and garlic for 3–4 minutes.

Cut the braising beef into chunks and cook over high heat for 3 minutes until browned all over. Add the paprika and stir well, then add the chopped tomatoes, tomato paste, bell pepper, and mushrooms. Cook for 2 minutes, stirring frequently.

Pour in the beef stock. Bring to a boil, then reduce the heat. Cover and simmer for 1½–2 hours until the meat is tender.

Blend the cornstarch with the water, then add to the pan, stirring until thickened and smooth. Cook for 1 minute, then season with salt and pepper to taste.

Put the yogurt in a serving bowl and sprinkle with a little paprika.

Transfer the beef goulash to a warmed serving dish, garnish with chopped fresh parsley, and serve with the yogurt and freshly cooked long-grain and wild rice.

SERVES 4

2 tbsp vegetable oil

1 large onion, chopped

1 garlic clove, crushed

1 lb 10 oz/750 g lean braising beef

2 tbsp paprika

15 oz/425 g can chopped tomatoes

2 tbsp tomato paste

1 large red bell pepper, seeded and chopped

6 oz/175 g button mushrooms, sliced

2½ cups beef stock

1 tbsp cornstarch

1 tbsp water

salt and pepper

4 tbsp lowfat plain yogurt

paprika, for sprinkling

chopped fresh parsley, to garnish

freshly cooked long-grain and wild rice, to serve

BEEF WITH HERBS & VEGETABLES

Preheat the oven to 375°F/190°C. To make the stock, trim as much fat as possible from the beef and put in a large roasting pan with the bones and onions. Roast for 30–40 minutes until browned, turning once or twice. Transfer the ingredients to a large flameproof casserole and discard the fat.

Add the water (it should cover by at least 2 inches/5 cm) and bring to a boil. Skim off any foam that rises to the surface. Reduce the heat and add the garlic, carrots, leek, celery, bay leaf, thyme, and a pinch of salt. Simmer very gently, uncovered, for 4 hours, skimming occasionally. Do not stir. If the ingredients emerge from the liquid, top up with water.

Gently ladle the stock through a cheesecloth-lined sieve into a large container and remove as much fat as possible. Save the meat for another purpose, if desired, and discard the bones and vegetables. (There should be about 8 cups of stock.)

Boil the stock very gently until it is reduced to 6¼ cups, or if the stock already has concentrated flavor, measure out that amount and save the rest for another purpose. Taste the stock and adjust the seasoning if necessary.

Bring a saucepan of salted water to a boil and drop in the celeriac and carrots. Reduce the heat, cover, and boil gently for about 15 minutes until tender. Drain.

Add the marjoram and parsley to the boiling beef stock. Divide the cooked vegetables and diced tomatoes among warmed bowls, ladle over the boiling stock, and serve.

SERVES 4–6

- 7 oz/200 g celeriac, peeled and finely diced
- 2 large carrots, finely diced
- 2 tsp chopped fresh marjoram leaves
- 2 tsp chopped fresh parsley
- 2 plum tomatoes, skinned, seeded, and diced
- salt and pepper

beef stock

- 1 lb 4 oz/550 g boneless beef shin or braising beef, cut into large cubes
- 1 lb 10 oz/750 g veal, beef, or pork bones
- 2 onions, quartered
- 10 cups water
- 4 garlic cloves, sliced
- 2 carrots, sliced
- 1 large leek, sliced
- 1 celery stick, chopped
- 1 bay leaf
- 4–5 sprigs of fresh thyme, or ¼ tsp dried thyme
- salt

PEPPER POT-STYLE STEW

SERVES 4

1 lb/450 g braising beef
1½ tbsp all-purpose flour
2 tbsp olive oil
1 red onion, chopped
3–4 garlic cloves, crushed
1 fresh green chile, seeded and chopped
3 celery stalks, sliced
4 whole cloves
1 tsp ground allspice
1–2 tsp hot pepper sauce, or to taste
2½ cups beef stock
8 oz/225 g seeded and peeled squash, such as acorn, cut into small chunks
1 large red bell pepper, seeded and chopped
4 tomatoes, coarsely chopped
4 oz/115 g okra, trimmed and halved
freshly cooked wild rice, to serve

Trim any fat or gristle from the beef and cut the meat into 1-inch/2.5-cm chunks. Toss the beef in the flour until well coated and reserve any remaining flour.

Heat the oil in a large, heavy-bottom pan and cook the onion, garlic, chile, and celery with the cloves and allspice, stirring frequently, for 5 minutes or until softened. Add the beef and cook over high heat, stirring frequently, for 3 minutes, or until browned on all sides and seared. Sprinkle in the reserved flour and cook, stirring constantly, for 2 minutes, then remove from the heat.

Add the hot pepper sauce and gradually stir in the stock, then return to the heat and bring to a boil, stirring. Reduce the heat, then cover and simmer, stirring occasionally, for 1½ hours.

Add the squash and red bell pepper to the pan and simmer for an additional 15 minutes. Add the tomatoes and okra and simmer for an additional 15 minutes, or until the beef is tender. Serve with the wild rice.

BEEF & VEGETABLE STEW

Trim any fat or gristle from the beef and cut the meat into
1-inch/2.5-cm chunks. Mix the flour and spices together.
Toss the beef in the spiced flour until well coated.

Heat the oil in a large, heavy-bottom pan and cook the
onion, garlic, and celery, stirring frequently, for 5 minutes
or until softened. Add the beef and cook over high heat,
stirring frequently, for 3 minutes, or until browned on all
sides and seared.

Add the carrots, then remove from the heat. Gradually stir
in the lager and stock, then return to the heat and bring to a
boil, stirring. Reduce the heat, then cover and simmer, stirring
occasionally, for 1½ hours.

Add the potatoes to the pan and simmer for an additional
15 minutes. Add the red bell pepper and corn cobs and simmer
for 15 minutes, then add the tomatoes and peas and simmer
for an additional 10 minutes, or until the beef and vegetables
are tender. Season to taste with salt and pepper, then stir in the
cilantro and serve.

SERVES 4

1 lb/450 g braising beef
1½ tbsp all-purpose flour
1 tsp hot paprika
1–1½ tsp chili powder
1 tsp ground ginger
2 tbsp olive oil
1 large onion, cut into chunks
3 garlic cloves, sliced
2 celery stalks, sliced
8 oz/225 g carrots, chopped
1¼ cups lager
1¼ cups beef stock
12 oz/350 g potatoes, chopped
1 red bell pepper, seeded and
   chopped
2 corn cobs, halved
4 oz/115 g tomatoes, cut into
   quarters
1 cup shelled fresh or frozen peas
salt and pepper
1 tbsp chopped fresh cilantro

RICH BEEF STEW

Combine the wine, brandy, vinegar, shallots, carrots, garlic, peppercorns, thyme, rosemary, parsley, and bay leaf, and season to taste with salt. Add the beef, stirring to coat, then cover with plastic wrap and marinate in the refrigerator for 8 hours, or overnight.

Preheat the oven to 300°F/150°C. Drain the beef, reserving the marinade, and pat dry on paper towels. Heat half the oil in a large, flameproof casserole. Add the beef cubes in batches and cook over medium heat, stirring, for 3–4 minutes, or until browned. Transfer the beef to a plate with a slotted spoon. Brown the remaining beef, adding more oil, if necessary.

Return all of the beef to the casserole and add the tomatoes and their juices, mushrooms, and orange rind. Strain the reserved marinade into the casserole. Bring to a boil, cover, and cook in the oven for 2½ hours.

Remove the casserole from the oven, add the prosciutto and olives, and return it to the oven to cook for an additional 30 minutes, or until the beef is very tender. Discard the orange rind and serve straight from the casserole, garnished with parsley.

SERVES 6

1½ cups dry white wine

2 tbsp brandy

1 tbsp white wine vinegar

4 shallots, sliced

4 carrots, sliced

1 garlic clove, finely chopped

6 black peppercorns

4 fresh thyme sprigs

1 fresh rosemary sprig

2 fresh parsley sprigs, plus extra to garnish

1 bay leaf

1 lb 10 oz/750 g top round steak, cut into 1-inch/2.5-cm cubes

2 tbsp olive oil

1 lb 12 oz/800 g canned chopped tomatoes

8 oz/225 g portobello mushrooms, sliced

strip of finely pared orange rind

2 oz/55 g prosciutto, cut into strips

12 black olives

salt

BEEF IN BEER WITH HERB DUMPLINGS

SERVES 6

2 tbsp corn oil

2 large onions, thinly sliced

8 carrots, sliced

4 tbsp all-purpose flour

2 lb 12 oz/1.25 kg braising beef, cut into cubes

generous 1¾ cups stout

2 tsp brown sugar

2 bay leaves

1 tbsp chopped fresh thyme

salt and pepper

herb dumplings

generous ¾ cup self-rising flour

pinch of salt

½ cup lard, chilled and cut into small pieces

2 tbsp chopped fresh parsley, plus extra to garnish

about 4 tbsp water

Preheat the oven to 325°F/160°C. Heat the oil in a flameproof casserole. Add the onions and carrots and cook over low heat, stirring occasionally, for 5 minutes, or until the onions are softened. Meanwhile, place the flour in a plastic bag and season with salt and pepper. Add the braising beef to the bag, tie the top, and shake well to coat. Do this in batches, if necessary.

Remove the vegetables from the casserole with a slotted spoon and reserve. Add the braising beef to the casserole, in batches, and cook, stirring frequently, until browned all over. Return all the meat and the onions and carrots to the casserole and sprinkle in any remaining seasoned flour. Pour in the stout and add the sugar, bay leaves, and thyme. Bring to a boil, cover, and transfer to the preheated oven to bake for 1¾ hours.

To make the herb dumplings, sift the flour and salt into a bowl. Stir in the suet and parsley and add enough of the water to make a soft dough. Shape into small balls between the palms of your hands. Add to the casserole and return to the oven for 30 minutes. Remove and discard the bay leaves and serve, sprinkled with parsley.

BEEF CHOP SUEY

Combine all the marinade ingredients in a bowl and marinate the beef for at least 20 minutes. Blanch the broccoli in a large pan of boiling water for 30 seconds. Drain and set aside.

In a preheated wok or deep skillet, heat 1 tablespoon of the oil and stir-fry the beef until the color has changed. Remove and set aside. Wipe out the wok or skillet with paper towels.

In the clean wok or deep pan, heat the remaining oil and stir-fry the onion for 1 minute. Add the celery and broccoli and cook for 2 minutes. Add the snow peas, bamboo shoots, water chestnuts, and mushrooms, and cook for 1 minute. Add the beef, then season with the oyster sauce and salt and serve.

SERVES 4

- 1 lb/450 g porterhouse steak, thinly sliced
- 1 head of broccoli, cut into small florets
- 2 tbsp vegetable oil or peanut oil
- 1 onion, thinly sliced
- 2 celery stalks, thinly sliced diagonally
- 2 cups snow peas, sliced in half lengthwise
- ½ cup fresh or canned bamboo shoots, rinsed and julienned (if using fresh shoots, boil in water first for 30 minutes)
- 8 water chestnuts, thinly sliced
- 4 cups thinly sliced button mushrooms
- 1 tbsp oyster sauce
- 1 tsp salt

marinade
- 1 tbsp Chinese rice wine
- pinch of white pepper
- pinch of salt
- 1 tbsp light soy sauce
- ½ tsp sesame oil

POT-ROAST PORK

Heat the oil with half the butter in a heavy-bottomed pan or flameproof casserole. Add the pork and cook over medium heat, turning frequently, for 5–10 minutes, or until browned. Transfer to a plate.

Add the shallots to the pan and cook, stirring frequently, for 5 minutes, or until softened. Add the juniper berries and thyme sprigs and return the pork to the pan, with any juices that have collected on the plate. Pour in the cider and stock, season to taste with salt and pepper, then cover and simmer for 30 minutes. Turn the pork over and add the celery. Re-cover the pan and cook for an additional 40 minutes.

Meanwhile, make a beurre manié by mashing the remaining butter with the flour in a small bowl. Transfer the pork and celery to a platter with a slotted spoon and keep warm. Remove and discard the juniper berries and thyme. Whisk the beurre manié, a little at a time, into the simmering cooking liquid. Cook, stirring constantly, for 2 minutes, then stir in the cream and bring to a boil.

Slice the pork and spoon a little of the sauce over it. Garnish with thyme sprigs and serve immediately with the celery, peas, and remaining sauce.

SERVES 4

1 tbsp corn oil

¼ cup butter

2 lb 4 oz/1 kg boned and rolled pork loin

4 shallots, chopped

6 juniper berries

2 fresh thyme sprigs, plus extra to garnish

⅔ cup hard cider

⅔ cup chicken stock or water

8 celery stalks, chopped

2 tbsp all-purpose flour

⅔ cup heavy cream

salt and pepper

freshly cooked peas, to serve

PORK & VEGETABLE BROTH

SERVES 4

1 tbsp chili oil

1 garlic clove, chopped

3 scallions, sliced

1 red bell pepper, seeded and finely sliced

2 tbsp cornstarch

4 cups vegetable stock

1 tbsp soy sauce

2 tbsp rice wine or dry sherry

5¼ oz/150 g pork tenderloin, sliced

1 tbsp finely chopped lemongrass

1 small red chile, seeded and finely chopped

1 tbsp grated fresh ginger

4 oz/115 g fine egg noodles

7 oz/200 g canned water chestnuts, drained and sliced

salt and pepper

Heat the oil in a large pan. Add the garlic and scallions and cook over medium heat, stirring, for 3 minutes, until slightly softened. Add the bell pepper and cook for an additional 5 minutes, stirring.

In a bowl, mix the cornstarch with enough of the stock to make a smooth paste and stir it into the pan. Cook, stirring, for 2 minutes. Stir in the remaining stock with the soy sauce and rice wine, then add the pork, lemongrass, chile, and ginger. Season with salt and pepper. Bring to a boil, then lower the heat and simmer for 25 minutes.

Bring a separate pan of water to a boil, add the noodles, and cook for 3 minutes. Remove from the heat, drain, then add the noodles to the soup along with the water chestnuts. Cook for another 2 minutes, then remove from the heat and ladle into serving bowls.

MEAT

PORK CHOPS WITH BELL PEPPERS & CORN

Heat the oil in a large, flameproof casserole. Add the pork chops in batches and cook over medium heat, turning occasionally, for 5 minutes, or until browned. Transfer the chops to a plate with a slotted spoon.

Add the chopped onion to the casserole and cook, stirring occasionally, for 5 minutes, or until softened. Add the garlic and bell peppers and cook, stirring occasionally, for an additional 5 minutes. Stir in the corn kernels and their juices and the parsley and season to taste.

Return the chops to the casserole, spooning the vegetable mixture over them. Cover and simmer for 30 minutes, or until tender. Serve immediately with mashed potatoes.

SERVES 4

1 tbsp corn oil

4 pork chops, trimmed of visible fat

1 onion, chopped

1 garlic clove, finely chopped

1 green bell pepper, seeded and sliced

1 red bell pepper, seeded and sliced

11½ oz/325 g canned corn kernels

1 tbsp chopped fresh parsley

salt and pepper

mashed potatoes, to serve

PORK & VEGETABLE STEW

Trim off any fat or gristle from the pork and cut the meat into thin strips about 2-inches/5-cm long. Mix the flour and spices together. Toss the pork in the spiced flour until well coated and reserve any remaining spiced flour.

Heat the oil in a large, heavy-bottom pan and cook the onion, stirring frequently, for 5 minutes, or until softened. Add the pork and cook over high heat, stirring frequently, for 5 minutes, or until browned on all sides and seared. Sprinkle in the reserved spiced flour and cook, stirring constantly, for 2 minutes, then remove from the heat.

Gradually add the tomatoes to the pan. Blend the tomato paste with a little of the stock in a pitcher and gradually stir into the pan, then stir in half the remaining stock.

Add the carrots, then return to the heat and bring to a boil, stirring. Reduce the heat, then cover and simmer, stirring occasionally, for 1½ hours. Add the squash and cook for an additional 15 minutes.

Add the leeks and okra, and the remaining stock if you prefer a thinner stew. Simmer for an additional 15 minutes, or until the pork and vegetables are tender. Season to taste with salt and pepper, then garnish with fresh parsley and serve with couscous.

SERVES 4

1 lb/450 g lean boneless pork

1½ tbsp all-purpose flour

1 tsp ground coriander

1 tsp ground cumin

1½ tsp ground cinnamon

1 tbsp olive oil

1 onion, chopped

14 oz/400 g canned chopped tomatoes

2 tbsp tomato paste

1¼–scant 2 cups chicken stock

8 oz/225 g carrots, chopped

12 oz/350 g squash, such as kabocha, peeled, seeded, and chopped

8 oz/225 g leeks, sliced, blanched, and drained

4 oz/115 g okra, trimmed and sliced

salt and pepper

sprigs of fresh parsley, to garnish

couscous, to serve

PORK WITH RED CABBAGE

SERVES 4

1 tbsp corn oil

1 lb 10 oz/750 g boned and rolled pork loin

1 onion, finely chopped

1 lb 2 oz/500 g red cabbage, thick stems removed and leaves shredded

2 large cooking apples, peeled, cored, and sliced

3 cloves

1 tsp brown sugar

3 tbsp lemon juice, and a thinly pared strip of lemon rind

lemon wedges, to garnish

Preheat the oven to 325°F/160°C. Heat the oil in a flameproof casserole. Add the pork and cook over medium heat, turning frequently, for 5–10 minutes, until browned. Transfer to a plate.

Add the chopped onion to the casserole and cook over low heat, stirring occasionally, for 5 minutes, or until softened. Add the cabbage, in batches, and cook, stirring, for 2 minutes. Transfer each batch (mixed with some onion) into a bowl with a slotted spoon.

Add the apple slices, cloves, and sugar to the bowl and mix well, then place about half the mixture in the bottom of the casserole. Top with the pork, then add the remaining cabbage mixture. Sprinkle in the lemon juice and add the strip of rind. Cover and cook in the preheated oven for 1½ hours.

Transfer the pork to a plate. Transfer the cabbage mixture to the plate with a slotted spoon and keep warm. Bring the cooking juices to a boil over high heat and reduce slightly. Slice the pork and arrange on warmed serving plates, surrounded with the cabbage mixture. Spoon the cooking juices over the meat and serve with wedges of lemon.

PAPRIKA PORK

Cut the pork into 1½-inch/4-cm cubes. Heat the oil and butter in a large pan. Add the pork and cook over medium heat, stirring, for 5 minutes, or until browned. Transfer to a plate with a slotted spoon.

Add the chopped onion to the pan and cook, stirring occasionally, for 5 minutes, or until softened. Stir in the paprika and flour and cook, stirring constantly, for 2 minutes. Gradually stir in the stock and bring to a boil, stirring constantly.

Return the pork to the pan, add the sherry and sliced mushrooms, and season to taste with salt and pepper. Cover and simmer gently for 20 minutes, or until the pork is tender. Stir in the sour cream and serve.

SERVES 4

1 lb 8 oz/675 g pork tenderloin

2 tbsp corn oil

2 tbsp butter

1 onion, chopped

1 tbsp paprika

2½ tbsp all-purpose flour

1¼ cups chicken stock, or 1 chicken bouillon cube dissolved in 1¼ cups boiling water

4 tbsp dry sherry

4 oz/115 g button mushrooms, sliced

salt and pepper

⅔ cup sour cream

SAUSAGE & BEAN CASSEROLE

Prick the sausages all over with a fork. Heat 2 tablespoons of the oil in a large, heavy-bottom skillet. Add the sausages and cook over low heat, turning frequently, for 10–15 minutes, until evenly browned and cooked through. Remove them from the skillet and keep warm. Drain off the oil and wipe out the skillet with paper towels.

Heat the remaining oil in the skillet. Add the onion, garlic, and bell pepper to the skillet and cook for 5 minutes, stirring occasionally, or until softened.

Add the tomatoes to the skillet and let the mixture simmer for about 5 minutes, stirring occasionally, or until slightly reduced and thickened.

Stir the sun-dried tomato paste, cannellini beans, and Italian sausages into the mixture in the skillet. Cook for 4–5 minutes or until the mixture is piping hot. Add 4–5 tablespoons of water if the mixture becomes too dry during cooking.

Transfer the sausage and bean casserole to serving plates and serve with mashed potatoes.

SERVES 4

8 Italian sausages

3 tbsp olive oil

1 large onion, chopped

2 garlic cloves, chopped

1 green bell pepper, seeded and sliced

8 oz/225 g fresh tomatoes, skinned and chopped, or 14 oz/400 g canned tomatoes, chopped

2 tbsp sun-dried tomato paste

14 oz/400 g can cannellini beans

4–5 tbsp water (optional)

mashed potatoes or rice, to serve

ASIAN PORK

SERVES 4

1 lb/450 g lean boneless pork

1½ tbsp all-purpose flour

1–2 tbsp olive oil

1 onion, cut into small wedges

2–3 garlic cloves, chopped

1-inch/2.5-cm piece fresh ginger, peeled and grated

1 tbsp tomato paste

1¼ cups chicken stock

8 oz/225 g canned pineapple chunks in natural juice

1–1½ tbsp dark soy sauce

1 red bell pepper, seeded and sliced

1 green bell pepper, seeded and sliced

1½ tbsp balsamic vinegar

4 scallions, diagonally sliced, to garnish

Trim off any fat or gristle from the pork and cut the meat into 1-inch/2.5-cm chunks. Toss the pork in the flour until well coated and reserve any remaining flour.

Heat the oil in a large, heavy-bottom pan and cook the onion, garlic, and ginger, stirring frequently, for 5 minutes, or until softened. Add the pork and cook over high heat, stirring frequently, for 5 minutes, or until browned on all sides and seared. Sprinkle in the reserved flour and cook, stirring constantly, for 2 minutes, then remove from the heat.

Blend the tomato paste with the stock in a heatproof pitcher and gradually stir into the pan. Drain the pineapple, reserving both the fruit and juice, and stir the juice into the pan.

Add the soy sauce to the pan, then return to the heat and bring to a boil, stirring. Reduce the heat, then cover and simmer, stirring occasionally, for 1 hour. Add the bell peppers and cook for an additional 15 minutes, or until the pork is tender. Stir in the vinegar and the reserved pineapple and heat through for 5 minutes. Serve sprinkled with the scallions.

SPICED PORK WITH BELL PEPPERS

Heat the oil in a wok or large skillet and sauté the onion and garlic for 1–2 minutes, until they are softened but not browned.

Add the pork slices and stir-fry for 2–3 minutes until browned all over. Add the bell pepper, mushrooms, and curry paste.

Dissolve the coconut in the stock and add to the wok with the soy sauce. Bring to a boil and then simmer for 4–5 minutes until the liquid has reduced and thickened.

Add the tomatoes and cilantro and cook for 1–2 minutes before serving with noodles.

SERVES 4

2 tbsp vegetable oil or peanut oil

1 onion, coarsely chopped

2 garlic cloves, chopped

1 lb/450 g pork tenderloin, thickly sliced

1 red bell pepper, seeded and cut into squares

6 oz/175 g button mushrooms, quartered

2 tbsp Thai red curry paste

4 oz/115 g block creamed coconut, chopped

1¼ cups pork stock or vegetable stock

2 tbsp Thai soy sauce

4 tomatoes, peeled, seeded, and chopped

handful of fresh cilantro, chopped

boiled noodles or rice, to serve

LAMB SHANKS
WITH HARISSA

Preheat the oven to 400°F/200°C. Prick the eggplants, place on a baking sheet, and bake for 1 hour. When cool, peel and chop.

Heat the oil in a large saucepan. Add the lamb and cook until browned. Add the onion, stock, and water. Bring to a boil. Reduce the heat and simmer for 1 hour.

For the harissa, process the bell peppers, coriander seeds, chiles, garlic, and caraway seeds in a food processor. With the motor running, add enough oil to make a paste. Season with salt, then spoon into a jar. Cover with oil, seal, and chill.

Remove the shanks from the stock, cut off the meat, and chop. Add the sweet potato, cinnamon, and cumin to the stock, bring to a boil, cover, and simmer for 20 minutes. Discard the cinnamon and process the mixture in a food processor with the eggplant. Return to the pan, add the lamb and cilantro, and heat until hot. Serve with the harissa.

SERVES 4

2 eggplants

3 tbsp olive oil

6 lamb shanks

1 small onion, chopped

1¾ cups chicken stock

8 cups water

14 oz/400 g sweet potato, cut into chunks

2-inch/5-cm piece cinnamon stick

1 tsp ground cumin

2 tbsp chopped fresh cilantro

harissa

2 red bell peppers, peeled, seeded, and chopped

½ tsp coriander seeds, dry-roasted

1 oz/25 g fresh red chiles, chopped

2 garlic cloves, chopped

2 tsp caraway seeds

olive oil

salt

LAMB PILAU

SERVES 4

2–3 tbsp vegetable oil

1 lb 7 oz/650 g boneless lamb
   shoulder, cut into 1-inch/2.5-cm
   cubes

2 onions, coarsely chopped

1 tsp ground cumin

7 oz/200 g risotto rice

1 tbsp tomato paste

1 tsp saffron threads

scant ½ cup pomegranate juice

scant 3½ cups lamb stock, chicken
   stock, or water

4 oz/115 g dried apricots or
   prunes, halved

2 tbsp raisins

2 tbsp shredded fresh mint

2 tbsp shredded fresh watercress

salt and pepper

Heat the oil in a large flameproof casserole or pan over high
heat. Add the lamb, in batches, and cook over high heat, turning
frequently, for 7 minutes, or until lightly browned.

Add the onions, reduce the heat to medium, and cook for
2 minutes, or until beginning to soften. Add the cumin and
rice and cook, stirring to coat, for 2 minutes, or until the rice is
translucent. Stir in the tomato paste and the saffron threads.

Add the pomegranate juice and stock. Bring to a boil, stirring.
Stir in the apricots and raisins. Reduce the heat to low, cover, and
simmer for 20–25 minutes, or until the lamb and rice are tender
and all of the liquid has been absorbed.

Season to taste with salt and pepper, then sprinkle the
shredded mint and watercress over the pilaf and serve straight
from the casserole.

MEAT

117

LAMB WITH PEARS

Preheat the oven to 325°F/160°C. Heat the olive oil in a flameproof casserole over medium heat. Add the lamb and cook, turning frequently, for 5–10 minutes, or until browned on all sides.

Arrange the pear pieces on top, then sprinkle over the ginger. Cover with the potatoes. Pour in the cider and season to taste with salt and pepper. Cover and cook in the preheated oven for 1¼ hours.

Trim the stem ends of the green beans. Remove the casserole from the oven and add the beans, then re-cover and return to the oven for an additional 30 minutes. Taste and adjust the seasoning and sprinkle with the chives. Serve immediately.

SERVES 4

1 tbsp olive oil

2 lb 4 oz/1 kg best end-of-neck lamb cutlets, trimmed of visible fat

6 pears, peeled, cored, and cut into quarters

1 tsp ground ginger

4 potatoes, diced

4 tbsp hard cider

1 lb/450 g green beans

salt and pepper

2 tbsp snipped fresh chives, to garnish

CINNAMON LAMB CASSEROLE

Season the flour with salt and pepper to taste and put it with the lamb in a plastic bag, then hold the top closed and shake until the lamb cubes are lightly coated all over. Remove the lamb from the bag, then shake off any excess flour and set aside.

Heat the oil in a large, flameproof casserole and cook the onions and garlic, stirring frequently, for 5 minutes, or until softened. Add the lamb and cook over high heat, stirring frequently, for 5 minutes, or until browned on all sides and seared.

Stir the wine, vinegar, and tomatoes and their juice into the casserole, scraping any sediment from the bottom of the casserole, and bring to a boil. Reduce the heat and add the raisins, cinnamon, sugar, and bay leaf. Season to taste with salt and pepper. Cover and simmer gently for 2 hours, or until the lamb is tender.

Meanwhile, make the topping. Put the yogurt into a small serving bowl, then stir in the garlic and season to taste with salt and pepper. Cover and chill in the refrigerator until ready to serve.

Discard the bay leaf and serve the lamb hot, topped with a spoonful of the garlic yogurt, and dusted with paprika.

SERVES 6

2 tbsp all-purpose flour

2 lb 4 oz/1 kg lean boneless lamb, cubed

2 tbsp olive oil

2 large onions, sliced

1 garlic clove, finely chopped

1¼ cups full-bodied red wine

2 tbsp red wine vinegar

14 oz/400 g canned chopped tomatoes

generous ⅓ cup seedless raisins

1 tbsp ground cinnamon

pinch of sugar

1 bay leaf

salt and pepper

paprika, to garnish

topping

⅔ cup plain yogurt

2 garlic cloves, crushed

salt and pepper

LAMB STEW WITH CHICKPEAS

SERVES 4–6

6 tbsp olive oil

8 oz/225 g chorizo sausage, cut into ¼-inch/5-mm thick slices, casings removed

2 large onions, chopped

6 large garlic cloves, crushed

2 lb/900 g boned leg of lamb, cut into 2-inch/5-cm chunks

scant 1¼ cups lamb stock or water

½ cup red wine, such as Rioja or Tempranillo

2 tbsp sherry vinegar

1 lb 12 oz/800 g canned chopped tomatoes

4 sprigs fresh thyme, plus extra to garnish

2 bay leaves

½ tsp sweet Spanish paprika

1 lb 12 oz/800 g canned chickpeas, rinsed and drained

salt and pepper

Heat 4 tablespoons of the oil in a large, heavy-bottom flameproof casserole over medium-high heat. Reduce the heat, add the chorizo, and cook for 1 minute; set aside. Add the onions to the casserole and cook for 2 minutes, then add the garlic and continue cooking for 3 minutes, or until the onions are soft, but not brown. Remove from the casserole and set aside.

Heat the remaining 2 tablespoons of oil in the casserole. Add the lamb chunks in a single layer without overcrowding the casserole, and cook until browned on all sides; work in batches, if necessary.

Return the onion mixture to the casserole with all the lamb. Stir in the stock, wine, vinegar, tomatoes with their juices, and salt and pepper to taste. Bring to a boil, scraping any glazed bits from the bottom of the casserole. Reduce the heat and stir in the thyme, bay leaves, and paprika.

Transfer to a preheated oven, 325°F/160°C, and cook, covered, for 40–45 minutes until the lamb is tender. Stir in the chickpeas and return to the oven, uncovered, for 10 minutes, or until they are heated through and the juices are reduced.

Taste and adjust the seasoning. Garnish with thyme and serve.

SPICY LAMB & CHICKPEA STEW

Heat 1 tablespoon of the oil in a large saucepan or cast-iron casserole over medium–high heat. Cut the lamb into cubes and add to the pan, in batches if necessary to avoid overcrowding, and cook until evenly browned on all sides, adding a little more oil if needed. Remove the meat with a slotted spoon when browned.

Reduce the heat and add the onion and garlic to the pan. Cook, stirring frequently, for 1–2 minutes.

Add the water and return all the meat to the pan. Bring just to a boil and skim off any foam that rises to the surface. Reduce the heat and stir in the tomatoes, bay leaf, thyme, oregano, cinnamon, cumin, turmeric, and harissa. Simmer for about 1 hour, or until the meat is very tender. Discard the bay leaf.

Rinse and drain the chickpeas, then stir into the pan with the carrot and potato and simmer for 15 minutes. Add the zucchini and peas and continue simmering for 15–20 minutes, or until all the vegetables are tender.

Adjust the seasoning, adding more harissa, if desired. Ladle the soup into warmed bowls and garnish with mint or cilantro.

SERVES 4–6

1–2 tbsp olive oil

1 lb/450 g lean boneless lamb

1 onion, finely chopped

2–3 garlic cloves, crushed

5 cups water

14 oz/400 g canned chopped tomatoes

1 bay leaf

½ tsp each dried thyme and oregano

⅛ tsp ground cinnamon

¼ tsp each ground cumin and turmeric

1 tsp harissa, or more to taste

14 oz/400 g canned chickpeas

1 carrot, diced

1 potato, diced

1 zucchini, quartered lengthwise and sliced

3½ oz/100 g fresh or defrosted frozen peas

salt and pepper

sprigs of fresh mint or cilantro, to garnish

IRISH STEW

Preheat the oven to 325°F/160°C. Spread the flour on a plate and season with salt and pepper. Roll the pieces of lamb in the flour to coat, shaking off any excess, and arrange in the bottom of a casserole.

Layer the onions, carrots, and potatoes on top of the lamb.

Sprinkle in the thyme and pour in the stock, then cover and cook in the preheated oven for 2½ hours. Garnish with the chopped parsley and serve straight from the casserole.

SERVES 4

4 tbsp all-purpose flour

3 lb/1.3 kg middle neck of lamb, trimmed of visible fat, cut into chunks

3 large onions, chopped

3 carrots, sliced

1 lb/450 g potatoes, cut into quarters

½ tsp dried thyme

scant 3½ cups hot beef stock

salt and pepper

2 tbsp chopped fresh parsley, to garnish

LAMB SHANKS

SERVES 6

1 tsp coriander seeds

1 tsp cumin seeds

1 tsp ground cinnamon

1 fresh green chile, seeded and
finely chopped

1 garlic bulb, separated into cloves

½ cup peanut oil or sunflower oil

grated rind of 1 lime

6 lamb shanks

2 onions, chopped

2 carrots, chopped

2 celery stalks, chopped

1 lime, chopped

3 cups beef stock or water

1 tsp sun-dried tomato paste

2 fresh mint sprigs

2 fresh rosemary sprigs, plus
extra to garnish

salt and pepper

Dry-roast the coriander and cumin seeds until fragrant, then
pound with the cinnamon, chile, and 2 garlic cloves in a mortar
and pestle. Stir in half the oil and the lime rind. Rub the spice
paste all over the lamb and marinate for 4 hours.

Preheat the oven to 400°F/200°C. Heat the remaining oil in
a flameproof casserole and cook the lamb, turning frequently,
until evenly browned. Chop the remaining garlic and add to the
casserole with the onions, carrots, celery, and lime, then pour in
enough stock or water to cover. Stir in the tomato paste, add the
herbs, and season with salt and pepper.

Cover and cook in the preheated oven for 30 minutes. Reduce
the oven temperature to 325°F/160°C and cook for an additional
3 hours, or until very tender.

Transfer the lamb to a dish. Strain the cooking liquid to remove
any solids, then return the liquid to the casserole. Boil until
reduced and thickened. Serve the lamb with the sauce poured
over it, garnished with sprigs of rosemary.

HEARTY WINTER BROTH

Heat the vegetable oil in a large, heavy-bottom saucepan and add the pieces of lamb, turning them to sear and brown on both sides. Lift the lamb out of the pan and set aside until ready to use.

Add the onion, carrots, and leeks to the saucepan and cook gently for about 3 minutes.

Return the lamb to the saucepan and add the vegetable stock, bay leaf, parsley, and pearl barley to the saucepan. Bring the mixture in the pan to a boil, then reduce the heat. Cover and simmer for 1½ –2 hours.

Discard the parsley sprigs and the bay leaf. Lift the pieces of lamb from the broth and let them cool slightly. Remove the bones and any fat and chop the meat. Return the lamb to the broth and reheat gently. Season to taste with salt and pepper.

It is advisable to prepare this soup a day ahead, then leave it to cool, cover, and refrigerate overnight. When ready to serve, remove and discard the layer of fat from the surface and reheat the soup gently. Ladle into warmed bowls and serve immediately.

SERVES 4

1 tbsp vegetable oil

1 lb 2 oz/500 g lean neck of lamb, cut into chunks

1 large onion, sliced

2 carrots, sliced

2 leeks, sliced

4 cups vegetable stock

1 bay leaf

sprigs of fresh parsley

2 oz/55 g pearl barley

salt and pepper

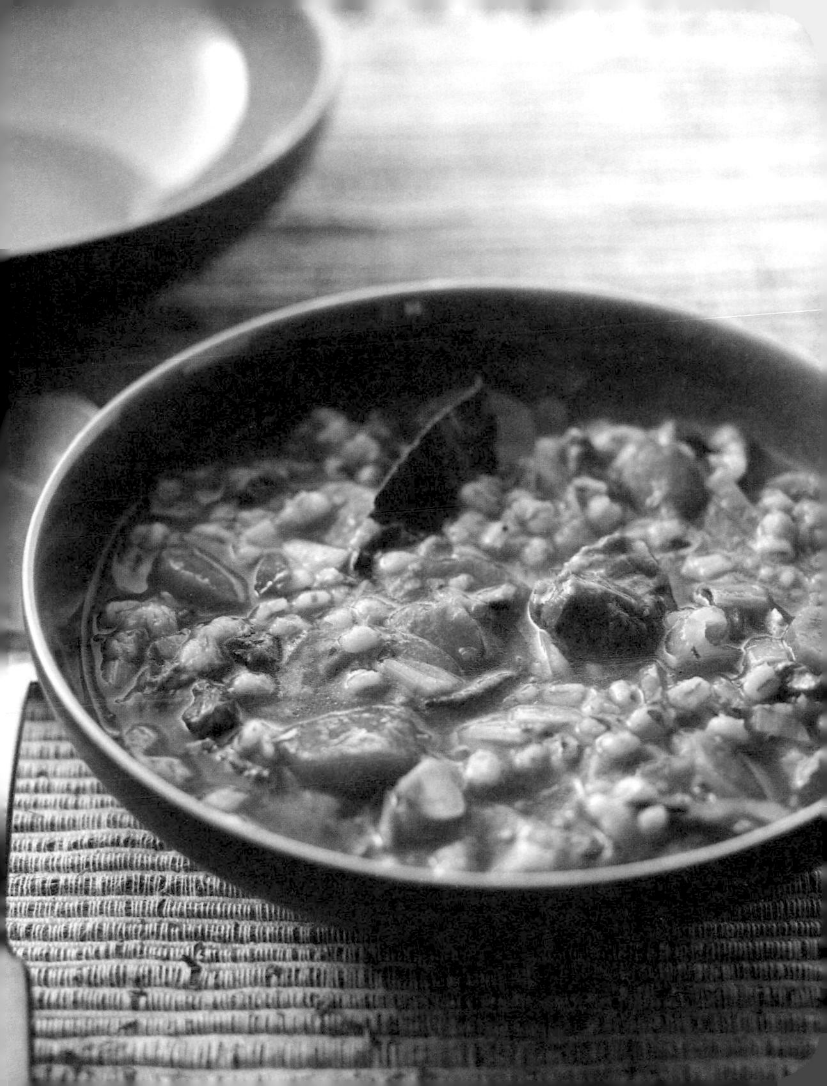

OSSO BUCCO

Heat the oil and butter in a large, heavy-bottom skillet. Add the onions and leek and cook over low heat, stirring occasionally, for 5 minutes, until softened.

Spread out the flour on a plate and season with salt and pepper. Toss the slices of veal in the flour to coat, shaking off any excess. Add the veal to the skillet, increase the heat to high, and cook until browned on both sides.

Gradually stir in the wine and stock and bring just to a boil, stirring constantly. Reduce the heat, cover, and simmer for 1¼ hours, or until the veal is very tender.

Meanwhile, make the gremolata by mixing the parsley, garlic, and lemon rind in a small bowl.

Transfer the veal to a warmed serving dish with a slotted spoon. Bring the sauce to a boil and cook, stirring occasionally, until thickened and reduced. Pour the sauce over the veal, sprinkle with the gremolata, and serve immediately.

SERVES 4

1 tbsp virgin olive oil

4 tbsp butter

2 onions, chopped

1 leek, sliced

3 tbsp all-purpose flour

4 thick slices of veal shin (osso bucco)

1¼ cups white wine

1¼ cups veal stock or chicken stock

salt and pepper

gremolata

2 tbsp chopped fresh parsley

1 garlic clove, finely chopped

grated rind of 1 lemon

POULTRY

ITALIAN-STYLE ROAST CHICKEN

Rinse the chicken inside and out with cold water and drain well. Carefully cut between the skin and the top of the breast meat using a small pointed knife. Slide a finger into the slit and carefully enlarge it to form a pocket. Continue until the skin is completely lifted away from both breasts and the top of the legs.

Chop the leaves from 3 rosemary stems. Mix with the feta cheese, sun-dried tomato paste, butter, and pepper to taste, then spoon under the skin. Put the chicken in a large roasting pan, cover with foil, and cook in a preheated oven, 375°F/190°C, for 20 minutes per 1 lb 2 oz/500 g, plus 20 minutes.

Break the garlic bulb into cloves but do not peel. Add the vegetables and garlic to the chicken after 40 minutes, drizzle with oil, tuck in a few stems of rosemary, and season with salt and pepper. Cook for the remaining calculated time, removing the foil for the last 40 minutes to brown the chicken.

Transfer the chicken to a serving platter. Place some of the vegetables around the chicken and transfer the remainder to a warmed serving dish. Spoon the fat (it will be floating on top) out of the roasting pan and stir the flour into the remaining cooking juices. Place the roasting pan on top of the stove and cook over medium heat for 2 minutes, then gradually stir in the stock. Bring to a boil, stirring, until thickened. Strain into a sauce boat and serve with the chicken.

SERVES 6

5 lb 8 oz/2.5 kg chicken

sprigs of fresh rosemary

¾ cup coarsely grated feta cheese

2 tbsp sun-dried tomato paste

4 tbsp butter, softened

1 bulb garlic

2 lb 4 oz/1 kg new potatoes, halved if large

1 each red, green, and yellow bell pepper, seeded and cut into chunks

3 zucchini, thinly sliced

2 tbsp olive oil

2 tbsp all-purpose flour

2½ cups chicken stock

salt and pepper

CHICKEN IN WHITE WINE

Preheat the oven to 325°F/160°C. Melt half the butter with the oil in a flameproof casserole. Add the bacon and cook over medium heat, stirring, for 5–10 minutes, or until golden brown. Transfer the bacon to a large plate. Add the onions and garlic to the casserole and cook over low heat, stirring occasionally, for 10 minutes, or until golden. Transfer to the plate. Add the chicken and cook over medium heat, stirring constantly, for 8–10 minutes, or until golden. Transfer to the plate.

Drain off any excess fat from the casserole. Stir in the wine and stock and bring to a boil, scraping any sediment off the bottom. Add the bouquet garni and season to taste. Return the bacon, onions, and chicken to the casserole. Cover and cook in the preheated oven for 1 hour. Add the mushrooms, re-cover, and cook for 15 minutes. Meanwhile, make a beurre manié by mashing the remaining butter with the flour in a small bowl.

Remove the casserole from the oven and set over medium heat. Remove and discard the bouquet garni. Whisk in the beurre manié, a little at a time. Bring to a boil, stirring constantly, then serve, garnished with fresh herb sprigs.

SERVES 4

¼ cup butter

2 tbsp olive oil

2 thick, rindless, lean bacon strips, chopped

4 oz/115 g pearl onions, peeled

1 garlic clove, finely chopped

4 lb/1.8 kg chicken pieces

1¾ cups dry white wine

1¼ cups chicken stock

1 bouquet garni

4 oz/115 g button mushrooms

2½ tbsp all-purpose flour

salt and pepper

fresh mixed herbs, to garnish

COQ AU VIN

SERVES 4

¼ cup butter

2 tbsp olive oil

4 lb/1.8 kg chicken pieces

4 oz/115 g rindless smoked bacon, cut into strips

4 oz/115 g pearl onions, peeled

4 oz/115 g cremini mushrooms, halved

2 garlic cloves, finely chopped

2 tbsp brandy

scant 1 cup red wine

1¼ cups chicken stock

1 bouquet garni

2 tbsp all-purpose flour

salt and pepper

bay leaves, to garnish

Melt half the butter with the olive oil In a large, flameproof casserole. Add the chicken and cook over medium heat, stirring, for 8–10 minutes, or until golden brown. Add the bacon, onions, mushrooms, and garlic.

Pour in the brandy and set it alight with a match or taper. When the flames have died down, add the wine, stock, and bouquet garni, and season to taste with salt and pepper. Bring to a boil, reduce the heat, and simmer gently for 1 hour, or until the chicken pieces are cooked through and tender. Meanwhile, make a beurre manié by mashing the remaining butter with the flour in a small bowl.

Remove and discard the bouquet garni. Transfer the chicken to a large plate and keep warm. Stir the beurre manié into the casserole, a little at a time. Bring to a boil, return the chicken to the casserole, and serve immediately, garnished with bay leaves.

SPICED CHICKEN STEW

Season the chicken pieces with salt and dust with paprika.

Heat the oil and butter in a flameproof casserole or large pan. Add the chicken pieces and cook over medium heat, turning, for 10–15 minutes, or until golden. Transfer to a plate with a slotted spoon.

Add the onion and bell peppers to the casserole. Cook over low heat, stirring occasionally, for 5 minutes, or until softened. Add the tomatoes, wine, stock, Worcestershire sauce, Tabasco sauce, and parsley and bring to a boil, stirring. Return the chicken to the casserole, cover, and simmer, stirring occasionally, for 30 minutes.

Add the corn and beans to the casserole, partially re-cover, and simmer for an additional 30 minutes. Place the flour and water in a small bowl and mix to make a paste. Stir a ladleful of the cooking liquid into the paste, then stir it into the stew. Cook, stirring frequently, for 5 minutes. Serve, garnished with parsley.

SERVES 6

4 lb/1.8 kg chicken pieces

2 tbsp paprika

2 tbsp olive oil

2 tbsp butter

1 lb/450 g onions, chopped

2 yellow bell peppers, seeded and chopped

14 oz/400 g canned chopped tomatoes

scant 1 cup dry white wine

generous 1¾ cups chicken stock

1 tbsp Worcestershire sauce

½ tsp Tabasco sauce

1 tbsp finely chopped fresh parsley

11½ oz/325 g canned corn kernels, drained

15 oz/425 g canned lima beans, drained and rinsed

2 tbsp all-purpose flour

4 tbsp water

salt

fresh parsley sprigs, to garnish

HUNTER'S CHICKEN

Preheat the oven to 325°F/160°C. Heat the butter and oil in a flameproof casserole and cook the chicken over medium–high heat, turning frequently, for 10 minutes, or until golden all over and seared. Using a slotted spoon, transfer to a plate.

Add the onions and garlic to the casserole and cook over low heat, stirring occasionally, for 10 minutes, or until softened and golden. Add the tomatoes with their juice, the herbs, sun-dried tomato paste, and wine, and season to taste with salt and pepper. Bring to a boil, then return the chicken portions to the casserole, pushing them down into the sauce.

Cover and cook in the preheated oven for 50 minutes. Add the mushrooms and cook for an additional 10 minutes, or until the chicken is tender and the juices run clear when a skewer is inserted into the thickest part of the meat. Serve immediately.

SERVES 4

1 tbsp unsalted butter

2 tbsp olive oil

4 lb/1.8 kg skinned chicken portions

2 red onions, sliced

2 garlic cloves, finely chopped

14 oz/400 g canned chopped tomatoes

2 tbsp chopped fresh flat-leaf parsley

6 fresh basil leaves, torn

1 tbsp sun-dried tomato paste

⅔ cup red wine

8 oz/225 g button mushrooms, sliced

salt and pepper

SUNSHINE CHICKEN

SERVES 4

1 lb/450 g skinless, boneless chicken

1½ tbsp all-purpose flour

1 tbsp olive oil

1 onion, cut into wedges

2 celery stalks, sliced

⅔ cup orange juice

1¼ cups chicken stock

1 tbsp light soy sauce

1–2 tsp clear honey

1 tbsp grated orange rind

1 orange bell pepper, seeded and chopped

8 oz/225 g zucchini, sliced into half moons

2 small corn cobs, halved, or 3½ oz/100 g baby corn

1 orange, peeled and segmented

salt and pepper

1 tbsp chopped fresh parsley, to garnish

Lightly rinse the chicken and pat dry with paper towels. Cut into bite-size pieces. Season the flour well with salt and pepper. Toss the chicken in the seasoned flour until well coated and reserve any remaining seasoned flour.

Heat the oil in a large, heavy-bottom skillet and cook the chicken over high heat, stirring frequently, for 5 minutes, or until golden on all sides and seared. Using a slotted spoon, transfer to a plate.

Add the onion and celery to the skillet and cook over medium heat, stirring frequently, for 5 minutes, or until softened. Sprinkle in the reserved seasoned flour and cook, stirring constantly, for 2 minutes, then remove from the heat. Gradually stir in the orange juice, stock, soy sauce, and honey followed by the orange rind, then return to the heat and bring to a boil, stirring.

Return the chicken to the skillet. Reduce the heat, then cover and simmer, stirring occasionally, for 15 minutes. Add the orange bell pepper with the zucchini and corn cobs and simmer for an additional 10 minutes, or until the chicken and vegetables are tender. Add the orange segments, then stir well and heat through for 1 minute. Serve garnished with the parsley.

CHICKEN &
BARLEY STEW

Heat the oil in a large pot over medium heat. Add the chicken and cook for 3 minutes, then turn over and cook on the other side for another 2 minutes. Add the stock, barley, potatoes, carrots, leek, shallots, tomato paste, and bay leaf. Bring to a boil, lower the heat, and simmer for 30 minutes.

Add the zucchini and chopped parsley, cover the pan, and cook for another 20 minutes, or until the chicken is cooked through. Remove the bay leaf and discard.

In a separate bowl, mix the flour with 4 tablespoons of water and stir into a smooth paste. Add it to the stew and cook, stirring, over low heat for another 5 minutes. Season to taste with salt and pepper.

Remove from the heat, ladle into individual serving bowls, and garnish with sprigs of fresh parsley.

SERVES 4

2 tbsp vegetable oil

8 small, skinless chicken thighs

generous 2 cups chicken stock

scant ½ cup pearl barley, rinsed and drained

7 oz/200 g small new potatoes, scrubbed and cut in half lengthwise

2 large carrots, peeled and sliced

1 leek, trimmed and sliced

2 shallots, sliced

1 tbsp tomato paste

1 bay leaf

1 zucchini, trimmed and sliced

2 tbsp chopped fresh flat-leaf parsley, plus extra sprigs to garnish

2 tbsp all-purpose flour

4 tbsp water

salt and pepper

CHICKEN WITH GARLIC

Sift the flour onto a large plate and season with paprika and salt and pepper to taste. Dredge the chicken pieces with the flour on both sides, shaking off the excess.

Heat 4 tablespoons of the oil in a large, deep skillet or flameproof casserole over medium heat. Add the garlic and cook, stirring frequently, for about 2 minutes to flavor the oil. Remove with a slotted spoon and set aside to drain on paper towels.

Add as many chicken pieces, skin-side down, as will fit in a single layer. (Work in batches if necessary, to avoid overcrowding the skillet, adding a little extra oil if necessary.) Cook for 5 minutes until the skin is golden brown. Turn over and cook for 5 minutes longer.

Pour off any excess oil. Return the garlic and chicken pieces to the skillet and add the chicken stock, wine, and herbs. Bring to a boil, then reduce the heat, cover, and simmer for 20–25 minutes, until the chicken is cooked through and tender and the garlic is very soft.

Transfer the chicken pieces to a serving platter and keep them warm. Bring the cooking liquid to a boil, with the garlic and herbs, and boil until reduced to about 1½ cups. Remove and discard the herbs. Taste and adjust the seasoning, if necessary.

Spoon the sauce and the garlic cloves over the chicken pieces. Garnish with the parsley and thyme, and serve.

SERVES 6

4 tbsp all-purpose flour

Spanish paprika, either hot or smoked sweet, to taste

1 large chicken, about 3 lb 12 oz/ 1.7 kg, cut into 8 pieces, then rinsed

4–6 tbsp olive oil

24 large garlic cloves, peeled and halved

scant 2 cups chicken stock

4 tbsp dry white wine, such as white Rioja

2 sprigs of fresh parsley, 1 bay leaf, and 1 sprig of fresh thyme, tied together

salt and pepper

fresh parsley and thyme leaves, to garnish

CHICKEN RISOTTO WITH SAFFRON

SERVES 4

4½ oz/125 g butter

2 lb/900 g skinless, boneless chicken breasts, thinly sliced

1 large onion, chopped

1 lb 2 oz/500 g risotto rice

⅔ cup white wine

1 tsp crumbled saffron threads

generous 5½ cups boiling chicken stock

¼ cup freshly grated Parmesan cheese

salt and pepper

Melt 2 oz/55 g of the butter in a deep pan, add the chicken and onion, and cook, stirring frequently, for 8 minutes, or until golden brown.

Add the rice and mix to coat in the butter. Cook, stirring constantly, for 2–3 minutes, or until the grains are translucent. Add the wine and cook, stirring constantly, for 1 minute until reduced.

Mix the saffron with 4 tablespoons of the hot stock. Add the liquid to the rice and cook, stirring constantly, until it is absorbed.

Gradually add the remaining hot stock, a ladleful at a time. Stir constantly and add more liquid as the rice absorbs each addition. Cook for 20 minutes, or until all the liquid is absorbed and the rice is creamy. Season to taste.

Remove the risotto from the heat and add the remaining butter. Mix well, then stir in the Parmesan until it melts. Spoon the risotto onto warmed plates and serve at once.

POULTRY

153

PAPPARDELLE WITH CHICKEN & PORCINI

Place the porcini in a small bowl, add the hot water, and let soak for 20 minutes. Meanwhile, place the tomatoes and their can juices in a heavy-bottom pan and break them up with a wooden spoon, then stir in the chile. Bring to a boil, reduce the heat, and simmer, stirring occasionally, for 30 minutes, or until reduced.

Remove the mushrooms from their soaking liquid with a slotted spoon, reserving the liquid. Strain the liquid through a coffee filter paper or cheesecloth-lined strainer into the tomatoes and simmer for an additional 15 minutes.

Meanwhile, heat 2 tablespoons of the olive oil in a heavy-bottom skillet. Add the chicken and cook, stirring frequently, until golden brown all over and tender. Stir in the mushrooms and garlic and cook for 5 minutes.

While the chicken is cooking, bring a large, heavy-bottom pan of lightly salted water to a boil. Add the pasta, return to a boil, and cook for 8–10 minutes, or until tender but still firm to the bite. Drain well, transfer to a warmed serving dish, drizzle with the remaining olive oil, and toss lightly. Stir the chicken mixture into the tomato sauce, season to taste with salt and pepper, and spoon onto the pasta. Toss lightly, sprinkle with parsley, and serve immediately.

SERVES 4

⅜ cup dried porcini mushrooms

¾ cup hot water

1 lb 12 oz/800 g canned chopped tomatoes

1 fresh red chile, seeded and finely chopped

3 tbsp olive oil

12 oz/350 g skinless, boneless chicken, cut into thin strips

2 garlic cloves, finely chopped

12 oz/350 g dried pappardelle

salt and pepper

2 tbsp chopped fresh flat-leaf parsley, to garnish

CHICKEN PEPPERONATA

Toss the chicken thighs in the flour, shaking off the excess.

Heat the oil in a wide skillet and fry the chicken quickly until seared and lightly browned, then remove from the pan.

Add the onion to the pan and gently fry until soft. Add the garlic, bell peppers, tomatoes, and oregano, then bring to a boil, stirring.

Arrange the chicken over the vegetables, season well with salt and pepper, then cover the pan tightly and simmer for 20–25 minutes or until the chicken is completely cooked and tender.

Taste and adjust the seasoning if necessary, garnish with oregano, and serve with crusty whole wheat bread.

SERVES 4

8 skinless chicken thighs

2 tbsp whole wheat flour

2 tbsp olive oil

1 small onion, thinly sliced

1 garlic clove, crushed

1 each large red, yellow, and green bell peppers, seeded and thinly sliced

14 oz/400 g canned chopped tomatoes

1 tbsp chopped fresh oregano, plus extra to garnish

salt and pepper

crusty whole wheat bread, to serve

SPICY CHICKEN WITH VEGETABLES

SERVES 4

5 tbsp corn oil

4 chicken pieces

6 tbsp all-purpose flour

1 onion, chopped

2 celery stalks, sliced

1 green bell pepper, seeded
   and chopped

2 garlic cloves, finely chopped

2 tsp chopped fresh thyme

2 fresh red chiles, seeded
   and finely chopped

14 oz/400 g canned chopped
   tomatoes

1¼ cups chicken stock

salt and pepper

lamb's lettuce and chopped fresh
   thyme, to garnish

Heat the oil in a large, heavy-bottom saucepan or flameproof casserole. Add the chicken and cook over medium heat, stirring, for 5–10 minutes or until golden. Transfer the chicken to a plate with a slotted spoon.

Stir the flour into the oil and cook over very low heat, stirring constantly, for 15 minutes, or until light golden. Do not let it burn. Immediately add the onion, celery, and green bell pepper and cook, stirring constantly, for 2 minutes. Add the garlic, thyme, and chiles and cook, stirring, for 1 minute.

Stir in the tomatoes and their juices, then gradually stir in the stock. Return the chicken pieces to the pan, cover, and simmer for 45 minutes, or until the chicken is cooked through and tender. Season to taste with salt and pepper, transfer to warmed serving plates, and serve immediately, garnished with some lamb's lettuce and a sprinkling of chopped thyme.

CHICKEN TAGINE

Heat the oil in a large pan over medium heat, add the onion and garlic and cook for 3 minutes, stirring frequently. Add the chicken and cook, stirring constantly, for an additional 5 minutes, or until seared on all sides. Add the cumin and cinnamon sticks to the pan halfway through searing the chicken.

Sprinkle in the flour and cook, stirring constantly, for 2 minutes. Add the eggplant, red bell pepper, and mushrooms and cook for an additional 2 minutes, stirring constantly.

Blend the tomato paste with the stock, stir into the pan, and bring to a boil. Reduce the heat and add the chickpeas and apricots. Cover and let simmer for 15–20 minutes, or until chicken is tender.

Season with salt and pepper to taste and serve at once, sprinkled with cilantro.

SERVES 4

1 tbsp olive oil

1 onion, cut into small wedges

2–4 garlic cloves, sliced

1 lb/450 g skinless, boneless chicken breast, diced

1 tsp ground cumin

2 cinnamon sticks, lightly bruised

1 tbsp whole wheat flour

8 oz/225 g eggplant, diced

1 red bell pepper, seeded and chopped

3 oz/85 g button mushrooms, sliced

1 tbsp tomato paste

2½ cups chicken stock

10 oz/280 g canned chickpeas, drained and rinsed

⅓ cup no-soak dried apricots, chopped

salt and pepper

1 tbsp chopped fresh cilantro, to garnish

BALTI CHICKEN

Heat the ghee in a large, heavy-bottom skillet. Add the onions and cook over low heat, stirring occasionally, for 10 minutes, or until golden. Add the sliced tomatoes, nigella seeds, peppercorns, cardamom, cinnamon stick, chili powder, garam masala, garlic paste, and ginger paste, and season with salt to taste. Cook, stirring constantly, for 5 minutes.

Add the chicken and cook, stirring constantly, for 5 minutes, or until well coated in the spice paste. Stir in the yogurt. Cover and let simmer, stirring occasionally, for 10 minutes.

Stir in the chopped cilantro, chiles, and lime juice. Transfer to a warmed serving dish, sprinkle with more chopped cilantro, and serve immediately.

SERVES 6

3 tbsp ghee or vegetable oil

2 large onions, sliced

3 tomatoes, sliced

½ tsp nigella seeds

4 black peppercorns

2 cardamom pods

1 cinnamon stick

1 tsp chili powder

1 tsp garam masala

1 tsp garlic paste

1 tsp ginger paste

1 lb 9 oz/700 g skinless, boneless chicken breasts or thighs, diced

2 tbsp plain yogurt

2 tbsp chopped fresh cilantro, plus extra to garnish

2 fresh green chiles, seeded and finely chopped

2 tbsp lime juice

salt

SPICY AROMATIC CHICKEN

SERVES 4

4–8 chicken pieces, skinned

½ lemon, cut into wedges

4 tbsp olive oil

1 onion, coarsely chopped

2 large garlic cloves, finely chopped

½ cup dry white wine

14 oz/400 g canned chopped tomatoes in juice

pinch of sugar

½ tsp ground cinnamon

½ tsp ground cloves

½ tsp ground allspice

14 oz/400 g canned artichoke hearts or okra, drained

8 black olives, pitted

salt and pepper

Rub the chicken pieces with the lemon. Heat the oil in a large, flameproof casserole or lidded skillet. Add the onion and garlic and cook for 5 minutes, until softened. Add the chicken pieces and cook for 5–10 minutes, until browned on all sides.

Pour in the wine and add the tomatoes with their juice, along with the sugar, cinnamon, cloves, allspice, and salt and pepper and bring to a boil. Cover the casserole and simmer for 45 minutes to 1 hour, until the chicken is tender.

Meanwhile, if using artichoke hearts, cut them in half. Add the artichokes and the olives to the casserole 10 minutes before the end of cooking, and continue to simmer until heated through. Serve hot.

THAI GREEN CHICKEN CURRY

Heat the oil in a preheated wok or large, heavy-bottom skillet. Add 2 tablespoons of the curry paste and stir-fry briefly until all the aromas are released.

Add the chicken, lime leaves, and lemongrass and stir-fry for 3–4 minutes, until the meat is starting to color. Add the coconut milk and eggplants and let simmer gently for 8–10 minutes, or until tender.

Stir in the fish sauce and serve at once, garnished with Thai basil sprigs and lime leaves.

SERVES 4

2 tbsp peanut oil or corn oil

2 tbsp Thai green curry paste

1 lb 2 oz/500 g skinless boneless chicken breasts, cut into cubes

2 kaffir lime leaves, coarsely torn

1 lemongrass stalk, finely chopped

1 cup canned coconut milk

16 baby eggplants, halved

2 tbsp Thai fish sauce

fresh Thai basil sprigs and thinly sliced kaffir lime leaves, to garnish

CHICKEN JALFREZI

Grind the cumin and coriander seeds in a mortar with a pestle, then reserve. Heat the mustard oil in a large, heavy-bottom skillet over high heat for 1 minute, or until it begins to smoke. Add the vegetable oil, reduce the heat, and add the onion and garlic. Cook for 10 minutes, or until golden.

Add the tomato paste, chopped tomatoes, turmeric, ground cumin and coriander seeds, chili powder, garam masala, and vinegar to the skillet. Stir the mixture until fragrant.

Add the red bell pepper and fava beans and stir for an additional 2 minutes, or until the bell pepper is softened. Stir in the chicken, and season to taste with salt, then simmer gently for 6–8 minutes, until the chicken is heated through and the beans are tender. Transfer to warmed serving bowls, garnish with cilantro sprigs, and serve with freshly cooked rice.

SERVES 4

½ tsp cumin seeds

½ tsp coriander seeds

1 tsp mustard oil

3 tbsp vegetable oil

1 large onion, finely chopped

3 garlic cloves, crushed

1 tbsp tomato paste

2 tomatoes, peeled and chopped

1 tsp ground turmeric

½ tsp chili powder

½ tsp garam masala

1 tsp red wine vinegar

1 small red bell pepper, seeded and chopped

4½ oz/125 g frozen fava beans

1 lb 2 oz/500 g cooked chicken, chopped

salt

fresh cilantro sprigs, to garnish

freshly cooked rice, to serve

JAMBALAYA

SERVES 4

2 tbsp vegetable oil

2 onions, coarsely chopped

1 green bell pepper, seeded and coarsely chopped

2 celery stalks, coarsely chopped

3 garlic cloves, finely chopped

2 tsp paprika

10½ oz/300 g skinless, boneless chicken breasts, chopped

3½ oz/100 g andouille or other smoked sausage, chopped

3 tomatoes, peeled and chopped

2 cups long-grain rice

3¾ cups hot chicken stock or fish stock

1 tsp dried oregano

2 bay leaves

12 large jumbo shrimp

4 scallions, finely chopped

2 tbsp chopped fresh parsley

salt and pepper

chopped fresh herbs, to garnish

Heat the vegetable oil in a large skillet over low heat. Add the onions, bell pepper, celery, and garlic and cook for 8–10 minutes until all the vegetables have softened. Add the paprika and cook for another 30 seconds. Add the chicken and sausages and cook for 8–10 minutes until lightly browned. Add the tomatoes and cook for 2–3 minutes until they have collapsed.

Add the rice to the pan and stir well. Pour in the hot stock, oregano, and bay leaves, and stir well. Cover and simmer for 10 minutes.

Add the shrimp and stir well. Cover again and cook for another 6–8 minutes until the rice is tender and the shrimp are cooked through.

Stir in the scallions and parsley, and season to taste with salt and pepper. Transfer to a large serving dish, garnish with chopped fresh herbs, and serve.

ITALIAN TURKEY CUTLETS

Heat the oil in a flameproof casserole or heavy-bottom skillet. Add the turkey scallops and cook over medium heat for 5–10 minutes, turning occasionally, until golden. Transfer to a plate.

Seed and slice the red bell peppers. Slice the onion, add to the skillet with the bell peppers, and cook over low heat, stirring occasionally, for 5 minutes, or until softened. Add the garlic and cook for an additional 2 minutes.

Return the turkey to the skillet and add the strained tomatoes, wine, and marjoram. Season to taste. Bring to a boil, then reduce the heat, cover, and simmer, stirring occasionally, for 25–30 minutes, or until the turkey is cooked through and tender.

Stir in the cannellini beans. Simmer for an additional 5 minutes. Sprinkle the breadcrumbs over the top and place under a preheated medium-hot broiler for 2–3 minutes, or until golden. Serve, garnished with basil.

SERVES 4

1 tbsp olive oil

4 turkey scallops or steaks

2 red bell peppers

1 red onion

2 garlic cloves, finely chopped

1¼ cups strained tomatoes

⅔ cup medium white wine

1 tbsp chopped fresh marjoram

14 oz/400 g canned cannellini beans, drained and rinsed

3 tbsp fresh white breadcrumbs

salt and pepper

fresh basil sprigs, to garnish

SPICED TURKEY

Preheat the oven to 325°F/160°C. Spread the flour on a plate and season with salt and pepper. Coat the turkey fillets in the seasoned flour, shaking off any excess.

Heat the oil in a flameproof casserole. Add the turkey fillets and cook over medium heat, turning occasionally, for 5–10 minutes, or until golden. Transfer to a plate with a slotted spoon.

Add the onion and bell pepper to the casserole. Cook over low heat, stirring occasionally, for 5 minutes, or until softened. Sprinkle in any remaining seasoned flour and cook, stirring constantly, for 1 minute. Gradually stir in the stock, then add the raisins, chopped tomatoes, chili powder, cinnamon, cumin, and chocolate. Season to taste with salt and pepper. Bring to a boil, stirring constantly.

Return the turkey to the casserole, cover, and cook in the preheated oven for 50 minutes. Serve immediately, garnished with sprigs of cilantro.

SERVES 4

6 tbsp all-purpose flour

4 turkey breast fillets

3 tbsp corn oil

1 onion, thinly sliced

1 red bell pepper, seeded and sliced

1¼ cups chicken stock

2 tbsp raisins

4 tomatoes, peeled, seeded, and chopped

1 tsp chili powder

½ tsp ground cinnamon

pinch of ground cumin

1 oz/25 g semisweet chocolate, finely chopped or grated

salt and pepper

sprigs of fresh cilantro, to garnish

DUCK LEGS
WITH OLIVES

SERVES 4

4 duck legs, all visible fat
   trimmed off

1 lb 12 oz/800 g canned tomatoes,
   chopped

8 garlic cloves, peeled but left
   whole

1 large onion, chopped

1 carrot, peeled and finely
   chopped

1 celery stalk, peeled and finely
   chopped

3 sprigs fresh thyme

generous ½ cup Spanish green
   olives in brine, stuffed with
   pimientos, garlic, or almonds,
   drained and rinsed

1 tsp finely grated orange rind

salt and pepper

Put the duck legs in the bottom of a flameproof casserole or
a large, heavy-bottom skillet with a tight-fitting lid. Add the
tomatoes, garlic, onion, carrot, celery, thyme, and olives, and stir
together. Season with salt and pepper to taste.

Turn the heat to high and cook, uncovered, until the ingredients
start to bubble. Reduce the heat to low, cover tightly, and let
simmer for 1¼–1½ hours, until the duck is very tender. Check
occasionally and add a little water if the mixture appears to be
drying out.

When the duck is tender, transfer it to a serving platter, cover,
and keep hot in a preheated warm oven. Leave the casserole
uncovered, increase the heat to medium, and cook, stirring, for
about 10 minutes until the mixture forms a sauce. Stir in the
orange rind, then taste and adjust the seasoning if necessary.

Mash the tender garlic cloves with a fork and spread over the
duck legs. Spoon the sauce over the top. Serve at once.

DUCK JAMBALAYA-STYLE STEW

Remove and discard the skin and any fat from the duck breasts. Cut the flesh into bite-size pieces.

Heat half the oil in a large, deep skillet and cook the duck, ham, and chorizo over high heat, stirring frequently, for 5 minutes, or until browned on all sides and seared. Using a slotted spoon, remove from the skillet and set aside.

Add the onion, garlic, celery, and chiles to the skillet and cook over medium heat, stirring frequently, for 5 minutes, or until softened. Add the green bell pepper, then stir in the stock, oregano, tomatoes, and hot pepper sauce.

Bring to a boil, then reduce the heat and return the duck, ham, and chorizo to the skillet. Cover and simmer, stirring occasionally, for 20 minutes, or until the duck and ham are tender.

Serve immediately, garnished with parsley and accompanied by salad greens and rice.

SERVES 4

4 duck breasts, about 5½ oz/ 150 g each

2 tbsp olive oil

8 oz/225 g piece ham, cut into small chunks

8 oz/225 g chorizo, outer casing removed, cut into chunks

1 onion, chopped

3 garlic cloves, chopped

3 celery stalks, chopped

1–2 fresh red chiles, seeded and chopped

1 green bell pepper, seeded and chopped

2½ cups chicken stock

1 tbsp chopped fresh oregano

14 oz/400 g canned chopped tomatoes

1–2 tsp hot pepper sauce, or to taste

chopped fresh parsley, to garnish

salad greens and freshly cooked long-grain rice, to serve

FISH & SEAFOOD

MONKFISH PARCELS

Preheat the oven to 375°F/190°C. Cut 4 large pieces of foil, about 9-inches/23-cm square. Brush lightly with a little of the oil, then divide the zucchini and bell pepper among them.

Rinse the fish fillets under cold running water and pat dry with paper towels. Cut them in half, then put 1 piece on top of each pile of zucchini and bell pepper. Cut the bacon slices in half and lay 3 pieces across each piece of fish. Season to taste with salt and pepper, drizzle over the remaining oil, and close up the packages. Seal tightly, transfer to an ovenproof dish, and bake in the preheated oven for 25 minutes.

Remove from the oven, open each foil package slightly, and serve with pasta and slices of olive bread.

SERVES 4

4 tsp olive oil

2 zucchini, sliced

1 large red bell pepper, peeled, seeded, and cut into strips

2 monkfish fillets, about 4½ oz/125 g each, skin and membrane removed

6 smoked lean bacon slices

salt and pepper

freshly cooked pasta and slices of olive bread, to serve

ROASTED MONKFISH

Preheat the oven to 400°F/200°C. Remove the central bone from the fish if not already removed and make small slits down each fillet. Cut 2 of the garlic cloves into thin slivers and insert into the fish. Place the fish on a sheet of wax paper, season with salt and pepper to taste, and drizzle over 1 tablespoon of the oil. Bring the top edges together. Form into a pleat and fold over, then fold the ends underneath, completely encasing the fish. Set aside.

Put the remaining garlic cloves and all the vegetables into a roasting pan and drizzle with the remaining oil, turning the vegetables so that they are well coated in the oil.

Roast in the preheated oven for 20 minutes, turning occasionally. Put the fish package on top of the vegetables and cook for an additional 15–20 minutes, or until the vegetables are tender and the fish is cooked.

Remove from the oven and open up the package. Cut the monkfish into thick slices. Arrange the vegetables on warmed serving plates, top with the fish slices, and sprinkle with the basil. Serve at once.

SERVES 4

- 1 lb 8 oz/675 g monkfish tail, skinned
- 4–5 large garlic cloves, peeled
- 3 tbsp olive oil
- 1 onion, cut into wedges
- 1 small eggplant, about 10½ oz/ 300 g, cut into chunks
- 1 red bell pepper, seeded, cut into wedges
- 1 yellow bell pepper, seeded, cut into wedges
- 1 large zucchini, about 8 oz/225 g, cut into wedges
- salt and pepper
- 1 tbsp shredded fresh basil, to garnish

MEDITERRANEAN SWORDFISH

SERVES 4

2 tbsp olive oil

1 onion, finely chopped

1 celery stalk, finely chopped

4 oz/115 g green olives, pitted

1 lb/450 g tomatoes, chopped

3 tbsp bottled capers, drained

4 swordfish steaks, about
    5 oz/140 g each

salt and pepper

fresh flat-leaf parsley sprigs,
    to garnish

Heat the oil in a large, heavy-bottom skillet. Add the onion and celery and cook over low heat, stirring occasionally, for 5 minutes, or until softened.

Meanwhile, coarsely chop half the olives. Stir the chopped and whole olives into the pan with the tomatoes and capers and season to taste with salt and pepper.

Bring to a boil, then reduce the heat, cover, and simmer gently, stirring occasionally, for 15 minutes.

Add the swordfish steaks to the pan and return to a boil. Cover and simmer, turning the fish once, for 20 minutes, or until the fish is cooked and the flesh flakes easily. Transfer the fish to serving plates and spoon the sauce over them. Garnish with parsley and serve immediately.

SICILIAN-STYLE TUNA

Whisk all the marinade ingredients together in a small bowl. Put the tuna steaks in a large, shallow dish and spoon over 4 tablespoons of the marinade, turning until well coated. Cover and let marinate in the refrigerator for 30 minutes. Set aside the remaining marinade.

Heat a stovetop ridged grill pan over high heat. Put the fennel and onions in a separate bowl, add the oil, and toss well to coat. Add to the grill pan and cook for 5 minutes on each side until just beginning to color. Transfer to 4 warmed serving plates, drizzle with the reserved marinade, and keep warm.

Add the tuna steaks to the grill pan and cook, turning once, for 4–5 minutes until firm to the touch but still moist inside. Transfer the tuna to the serving plates and serve at once with crusty rolls.

SERVES 4

4 tuna steaks, about 5 oz/ 140 g each

2 fennel bulbs, thickly sliced lengthwise

2 red onions, sliced

2 tbsp extra virgin olive oil

crusty rolls, to serve

marinade

½ cup extra virgin olive oil

4 garlic cloves, finely chopped

4 fresh red chiles, seeded and finely chopped

juice and finely grated rind of 2 lemons

4 tbsp finely chopped fresh flat-leaf parsley

salt and pepper

FISH STEW
WITH CIDER

Melt the butter in a large saucepan over medium–low heat. Add the leek and shallots and cook for about 5 minutes, stirring frequently, until they start to soften. Add the cider and bring to a boil.

Stir in the stock, potatoes, and bay leaf with a large pinch of salt (unless stock is salty) and bring back to a boil. Reduce the heat, cover, and cook gently for 10 minutes.

Put the flour in a small bowl and very slowly whisk in a few tablespoons of the milk to make a thick paste. Stir in a little more to make a smooth liquid.

Adjust the heat so the soup bubbles gently. Stir in the flour mixture and cook, stirring frequently, for 5 minutes. Add the remaining milk and half the cream. Continue cooking for about 10 minutes until the potatoes are tender.

Chop the sorrel finely and combine with the remaining cream. Stir the sorrel cream into the stew and add the fish. Continue cooking, stirring occasionally, for about 3 minutes, until the monkfish stiffens or the cod just begins to flake. Taste the stew and adjust the seasoning, if needed. Ladle into warmed bowls, remove the bay leaf, and serve.

SERVES 4

2 tsp butter

1 large leek, thinly sliced

2 shallots, finely chopped

½ cup hard cider

1¼ cups fish stock

9 oz/250 g potatoes, diced

1 bay leaf

4 tbsp all-purpose flour

¾ cup milk

¾ cup heavy cream

2 oz/55 g fresh sorrel leaves

12 oz/350 g skinless monkfish or cod fillet, cut into 1-inch/2.5-cm pieces

salt and pepper

CATALAN FISH STEW

SERVES 4–6

large pinch of saffron threads

4 tbsp almost boiling water

6 tbsp olive oil

1 large onion, chopped

2 garlic cloves, finely chopped

1½ tbsp chopped fresh thyme leaves

2 bay leaves

2 red bell peppers, seeded and coarsely chopped

1 lb 12 oz/800 g canned chopped tomatoes

1 tsp smoked paprika

1 cup fish stock

1 cup blanched almonds, toasted and finely ground

12–16 live mussels

12–16 live clams

1 lb 5 oz/600 g thick boned hake or cod fillets, skinned and cut into 2-inch/5-cm chunks

12–16 raw shrimp, shelled and deveined

salt and pepper

thick crusty bread, to serve

Put the saffron threads in a heatproof pitcher with the water and set aside for at least 10 minutes to infuse.

Heat the oil in a large, heavy-bottom flameproof casserole over medium-high heat. Reduce the heat to low and cook the onion, stirring occasionally, for 10 minutes, or until golden but not browned. Stir in the garlic, thyme, bay leaves, and red bell peppers and cook, stirring frequently, for 5 minutes, or until the bell peppers are softened and the onions have softened further.

Add the tomatoes and paprika and simmer, stirring frequently, for an additional 5 minutes.

Stir in the stock, the saffron and its soaking liquid, and the almonds and bring to a boil, stirring. Reduce the heat and simmer for 5–10 minutes, or until the sauce reduces and thickens. Season to taste with salt and pepper.

Meanwhile, clean the mussels and clams by scrubbing or scraping the shells and pulling out any beards that are attached to the mussels. Discard any with broken shells or any that refuse to close when tapped.

Gently stir the hake into the stew so that it doesn't break up, then add the shrimp, mussels, and clams. Reduce the heat to very low, then cover and simmer for 5 minutes, or until the hake is opaque, the mussels and clams have opened, and the shrimp have turned pink. Discard any mussels or clams that remain closed. Remove the bay leaf and serve immediately with plenty of thick crusty bread for soaking up the juices.

MEDITERRANEAN FISH STEW

Heat the oil in a large, flameproof casserole. Add the onion, saffron, thyme, and a pinch of salt. Cook over low heat, stirring occasionally, for 5 minutes, or until the onion has softened.

Add the garlic and cook for an additional 2 minutes, then add the drained tomatoes and pour in the stock and wine. Season to taste with salt and pepper, bring the mixture to a boil, then reduce the heat and simmer for 15 minutes.

Add the chunks of red snapper and monkfish and simmer for 3 minutes. Add the clams and squid and simmer for 5 minutes, or until the clam shells have opened. Discard any clams that remain closed. Tear in the basil and stir. Serve garnished with the extra basil leaves.

SERVES 4

- 2 tbsp olive oil
- 1 onion, sliced
- pinch of saffron threads, lightly crushed
- 1 tbsp chopped fresh thyme
- 2 garlic cloves, finely chopped
- 1 lb 12 oz/800 g canned chopped tomatoes, drained
- 8 cups fish stock
- ¾ cup dry white wine
- 12 oz/350 g red snapper or pompano fillets, cut into chunks
- 1 lb/450 g monkfish fillet, cut into chunks
- 1 lb/450 g fresh clams, scrubbed
- 8 oz/225 g squid rings
- 2 tbsp fresh basil leaves, plus extra to garnish
- salt and pepper

SHRIMP LAKSA

Shell and devein the shrimp. Put the fish stock, salt, and the shrimp heads, shells, and tails in a large saucepan over high heat and slowly bring to a boil. Lower the heat and simmer for 10 minutes, then remove from the heat. Transfer to a bowl and keep warm

Meanwhile, make the laksa paste. Put all the ingredients except the oil in a food processor and blend. With the motor running, slowly add up to 2 tablespoons of oil just until a paste forms. (If your food processor is too large to work efficiently with this small quantity, use a mortar and pestle, or make double the quantity and keep leftovers tightly covered in the refrigerator to use another time.)

Heat the oil in the cleaned large saucepan over high heat. Add the paste and stir-fry until it is fragrant. Strain the stock through a strainer lined with cheesecloth. Stir the stock into the laksa paste, along with the coconut milk, nam pla, and lime juice. Bring to a boil, then lower the heat, cover, and simmer for 30 minutes.

Meanwhile, soak the noodles in a large bowl with enough lukewarm water to cover for 20 minutes, until soft. Alternatively, cook according to the package instructions. Drain and set aside.

Add the shrimp and bean sprouts to the soup and continue simmering just until the shrimp turn opaque and curl. Divide the noodles among 4 bowls and ladle the soup over, making sure everyone gets an equal share of the shrimp. Garnish with the cilantro and serve.

SERVES 4

20–24 large raw unshelled shrimp

2 cups fish stock

pinch of salt

1 tsp peanut oil

2 cups coconut milk

2 tsp nam pla (Thai fish sauce)

½ tbsp lime juice

4 oz/115 g dried medium rice noodles

⅜ cup bean sprouts

sprigs of fresh cilantro, to garnish

laksa paste

6 fresh cilantro stalks with leaves

3 large garlic cloves, crushed

1 fresh red chile, seeded and chopped

1 lemongrass stalk, center part only, chopped

1-inch/2.5-cm piece fresh ginger, peeled and chopped

1½ tbsp shrimp paste

½ tsp ground turmeric

2 tbsp peanut oil

SHRIMP WITH COCONUT RICE

SERVES 4

1 cup dried Chinese mushrooms

2 tbsp vegetable oil or peanut oil

6 scallions, chopped

scant ½ cup dry unsweetened coconut

1 fresh green chile, seeded and chopped

generous 1 cup jasmine rice

⅔ cup fish stock

1¾ cups coconut milk

12 oz/350 g cooked shelled shrimp

6 sprigs fresh Thai basil

Place the mushrooms in a small bowl, cover with hot water, and set aside to soak for 30 minutes. Drain, then cut off and discard the stalks and slice the caps.

Heat 1 tablespoon of the oil in a wok and stir-fry the scallions, coconut, and chile for 2–3 minutes, until lightly browned. Add the mushrooms and stir-fry for 3–4 minutes.

Add the rice and stir-fry for 2–3 minutes, then add the stock and bring to a boil. Reduce the heat and add the coconut milk. Let simmer for 10–15 minutes, until the rice is tender. Stir in the shrimp and basil, heat through, and serve.

SHRIMP BIRYANI

Soak the saffron in the lukewarm water for 10 minutes. Put the shallots, garlic, spices, chile, and salt into a spice grinder or mortar and pestle and grind to a paste.

Heat the ghee in a saucepan and add the mustard seeds. When they start to pop, add the shrimp and stir over high heat for 1 minute. Stir in the spice mix, then the coconut milk and yogurt. Simmer for 20 minutes.

Spoon the shrimp mixture into serving bowls. Top with the freshly cooked basmati rice and drizzle over the saffron water. Serve, garnished with the almonds, scallion, and sprigs of cilantro.

SERVES 8

1 tsp saffron strands

4 tbsp lukewarm water

2 shallots, coarsely chopped

3 garlic cloves, crushed

1 tsp chopped ginger

2 tsp coriander seeds

½ tsp black peppercorns

2 cloves

seeds from 2 green
  cardamom pods

1 tsp ground turmeric

1 fresh green chile, chopped

½ tsp salt

2 tbsp ghee

1 tsp whole black mustard seeds

1 lb 2 oz/500 g raw jumbo shrimp

1¼ cups coconut milk

1¼ cups lowfat plain yogurt

freshly cooked basmati rice,
  to serve

to garnish
slivered almonds, toasted

1 scallion, sliced

sprigs of fresh cilantro

SHRIMP & CHICKEN PAELLA

Soak the mussels in lightly salted water for 10 minutes. Put the saffron threads and water in a small bowl or cup and let infuse for a few minutes. Meanwhile, put the rice in a strainer and rinse in cold water until the water runs clear. Set aside.

Heat 3 tablespoons of the oil in a 12-inch/30-cm paella pan or ovenproof casserole. Add the chicken thighs and cook over medium–high heat, turning frequently, for 5 minutes, or until golden and crispy. Using a slotted spoon, transfer to a bowl. Add the chorizo to the pan and cook, stirring, for 1 minute, or until beginning to crisp. Add to the chicken.

Heat the remaining oil in the pan and cook the onions, stirring frequently, for 2 minutes, then add the garlic and paprika and cook for an additional 3 minutes, or until the onions are soft but not browned.

Add the drained rice, beans, and peas and stir until coated in oil. Return the chicken and chorizo and any accumulated juices to the pan. Stir in the stock, saffron and its soaking liquid, and salt and pepper to taste and bring to a boil, stirring constantly. Reduce the heat to low and let simmer, uncovered and without stirring, for 15 minutes, or until the rice is almost tender and most of the liquid has been absorbed.

Arrange the mussels, shrimp, and red bell peppers on top, then cover and simmer, without stirring, for an additional 5 minutes, or until the shrimp turn pink and the mussels open. Discard any mussels that remain closed. Taste and adjust the seasoning if necessary. Sprinkle with the parsley and serve immediately.

SERVES 6–8

- 16 live mussels
- ½ tsp saffron threads
- 2 tbsp hot water
- generous 1¾ cups paella rice
- 6 tbsp olive oil
- 6–8 unboned, skin-on chicken thighs
- 5 oz/140 g Spanish chorizo sausage, sliced
- 2 large onions, chopped
- 4 large garlic cloves, crushed
- 1 tsp mild or hot Spanish paprika
- 3½ oz/100 g green beans, chopped
- generous ¾ cup frozen peas
- 5 cups fish stock
- 16 raw shrimp, shelled and deveined
- 2 red bell peppers, halved and seeded, then broiled, peeled, and sliced
- salt and pepper
- 1¼ oz/35 g fresh parsley, chopped, to garnish

MOULES MARINIÈRES

SERVES 4

4 lb 8 oz/2 kg live mussels
1¼ cups dry white wine
6 shallots, finely chopped
1 bouquet garni
pepper
4 bay leaves, to garnish
crusty bread, to serve

Clean the mussels by scrubbing or scraping the shells and pulling off any beards. Discard any with broken shells or any that refuse to close when tapped with a knife. Rinse the mussels under cold running water.

Pour the wine into a large, heavy-bottom pan, add the shallots and bouquet garni, and season to taste with pepper. Bring to a boil over medium heat. Add the mussels, cover tightly, and cook, shaking the pan occasionally, for 5 minutes. Remove and discard the bouquet garni and any mussels that remain closed. Divide the mussels among 4 soup plates with a slotted spoon. Tilt the casserole to let any sediment settle, then spoon the cooking liquid over the mussels. Garnish with the bay leaves and serve immediately with bread.

SQUID WITH PARSLEY & PINE NUTS

Place the golden raisins in a small bowl, cover with lukewarm water, and set aside for 15 minutes to plump up.

Meanwhile, heat the olive oil in a heavy-bottom pan. Add the parsley and garlic and cook over low heat, stirring frequently, for 3 minutes. Add the squid and cook, stirring occasionally, for 5 minutes.

Increase the heat to medium, pour in the wine, and cook until it has almost completely evaporated. Stir in the strained tomatoes and season to taste with chili powder and salt. Reduce the heat again, cover, and let simmer gently, stirring occasionally, for 45–50 minutes, until the squid is almost tender.

Drain the golden raisins and stir them into the pan with the pine nuts. Let simmer for an additional 10 minutes, then serve immediately garnished with the reserved chopped parsley.

SERVES 4

- ½ cup golden raisins
- 5 tbsp olive oil
- 2 tbsp chopped fresh flat-leaf parsley, plus extra to garnish
- 2 garlic cloves, finely chopped
- 1 lb 12 oz/800 g prepared squid, sliced, or squid rings
- ½ cup dry white wine
- 1 lb 2 oz/500 g strained tomatoes
- pinch of chili powder
- ¾ cup finely chopped pine nuts
- salt

SEARED SCALLOPS IN GARLIC BROTH

Combine the garlic cloves, celery, carrot, onion, peppercorns, parsley stems, and water in a saucepan with a good pinch of salt. Bring to a boil, reduce the heat, and simmer, partially covered, for 30–45 minutes.

Strain the stock into a bowl, clean the saucepan, then return the stock to the pan. Taste and adjust the seasoning, and keep hot.

If using sea scallops, slice in half to form 2 thinner rounds from each. (If the scallops are very large, slice them into 3 rounds.) Sprinkle with salt and pepper.

Heat the oil in a skillet over medium–high heat and cook the scallops on one side for 1–2 minutes, until lightly browned and the flesh becomes opaque.

Divide the scallops among 4 warmed shallow bowls, arranging them browned-side up. Ladle the soup over the scallops, then float a few cilantro leaves on top. Serve immediately.

SERVES 4

1 large garlic bulb (about 3½ oz/ 100 g), separated into unpeeled cloves

1 celery stalk, chopped

1 carrot, chopped

1 onion, chopped

10 peppercorns

5–6 parsley stems

5 cups water

8 oz/225 g large sea scallops

1 tbsp oil

salt and pepper

fresh cilantro leaves, to garnish

ROASTED SEAFOOD

SERVES 4

1 lb 5 oz/600 g new potatoes, scrubbed and parboiled for 10–15 minutes

3 red onions, cut into wedges

2 zucchini, cut into chunks

8 garlic cloves, peeled but left whole

2 lemons, cut into wedges

4 fresh rosemary sprigs

4 tbsp olive oil

12 oz/350 g unshelled raw shrimp

2 small raw squid, cut into rings

4 tomatoes, quartered

Preheat the oven to 400°F/200°C. Place the potatoes in a large roasting pan together with the onions, zucchini, garlic, lemons, and rosemary sprigs.

Pour over the oil and toss to coat all the vegetables in it. Roast in the oven for 30 minutes, turning occasionally, until the potatoes are tender.

Once the potatoes are tender, add the shrimp, squid, and tomatoes, tossing to coat them in the oil, and roast for 10 minutes. All the vegetables should be cooked through and slightly charred for full flavor. Transfer the roasted seafood and vegetables to warmed serving plates and serve hot.

SEAFOOD IN SAFFRON SAUCE

Clean the mussels and clams by scrubbing or scraping the shells and pulling out any beards that are attached to the mussels. Discard any with broken shells or any that refuse to close when tapped.

Heat the oil in a large, flameproof casserole and cook the onion with the saffron, thyme, and a pinch of salt over low heat, stirring occasionally, for 5 minutes, or until softened.

Add the garlic and cook, stirring, for 2 minutes. Add the tomatoes, wine, and stock, then season to taste with salt and pepper and stir well. Bring to a boil, then reduce the heat and simmer for 15 minutes.

Add the fish chunks and simmer for an additional 3 minutes. Add the mussels, clams, and squid rings and simmer for an additional 5 minutes, or until the mussels and clams have opened. Discard any that remain closed. Stir in the basil and serve immediately, accompanied by plenty of fresh bread to soak up the broth.

SERVES 4

8 oz/225 g live mussels

8 oz/225 g live clams

2 tbsp olive oil

1 onion, sliced

pinch of saffron threads

1 tbsp chopped fresh thyme

2 garlic cloves, finely chopped

1 lb 12 oz/800 g canned tomatoes, drained and chopped

¾ cup dry white wine

8 cups fish stock

12 oz/350 g red snapper fillets, cut into bite-size chunks

1 lb/450 g monkfish fillet, cut into bite-size chunks

8 oz/225 g raw squid rings

2 tbsp fresh shredded basil leaves

salt and pepper

fresh bread, to serve

SEAFOOD CHILI

Place the shrimp, scallops, monkfish chunks, and lime slices in a large, nonmetallic dish with ¼ teaspoon of the chili powder, ¼ teaspoon of the ground cumin, 1 tablespoon of the chopped cilantro, half the garlic, the fresh chile, and 1 tablespoon of the oil. Cover with plastic wrap and let marinate for up to 1 hour.

Meanwhile, heat 1 tablespoon of the remaining oil in a flameproof casserole or large, heavy-bottom pan. Add the onion, the remaining garlic, and the red and yellow bell peppers and cook over low heat, stirring occasionally, for 5 minutes, or until softened.

Add the remaining chili powder, the remaining cumin, the cloves, cinnamon, and cayenne, with the remaining oil if necessary, and season to taste with salt. Cook, stirring, for 5 minutes, then gradually stir in the stock and the tomatoes and their juices. Partially cover and simmer for 25 minutes.

Add the beans to the tomato mixture and spoon the fish and shellfish on top. Cover and cook for 10 minutes, or until the fish and shellfish are cooked through. Sprinkle with the remaining cilantro and serve.

SERVES 4

4 oz/115 g raw shrimp, peeled

9 oz/250 g prepared scallops, thawed if frozen

4 oz/115 g monkfish fillet, cut into chunks

1 lime, peeled and thinly sliced

1 tbsp chili powder

1 tsp ground cumin

3 tbsp chopped fresh cilantro

2 garlic cloves, finely chopped

1 fresh green chile, seeded and chopped

3 tbsp corn oil

1 onion, coarsely chopped

1 red and 1 yellow pepper, seeded and coarsely chopped

¼ tsp ground cloves

pinch of ground cinnamon

pinch of cayenne pepper

salt

1½ cups fish stock

14 oz/400 g canned chopped tomatoes

14 oz/400 g canned red kidney beans, drained and rinsed

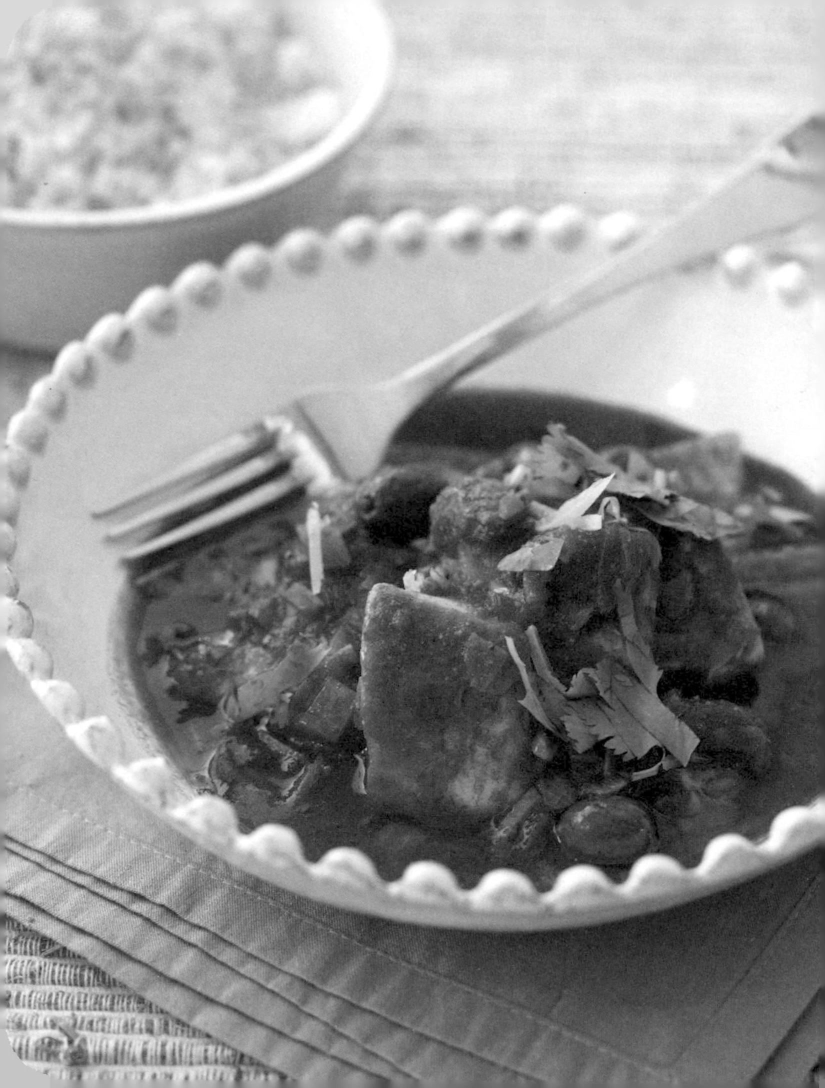

MOROCCAN FISH TAGINE

SERVES 4

2 tbsp olive oil

1 large onion, finely chopped

pinch of saffron threads

½ tsp ground cinnamon

1 tsp ground coriander

½ tsp ground cumin

½ tsp ground turmeric

7 oz/200 g canned chopped tomatoes

1¼ cups fish stock

4 small red snappers, cleaned, boned, and heads and tails removed

2 oz/55 g pitted green olives

1 tbsp chopped preserved lemon

3 tbsp chopped fresh cilantro

salt and pepper

freshly cooked couscous, to serve

Heat the olive oil in a flameproof casserole. Add the onion and cook gently over very low heat, stirring occasionally, for 10 minutes, or until softened, but not colored. Add the saffron, cinnamon, ground coriander, cumin, and turmeric and cook for an additional 30 seconds, stirring constantly.

Add the tomatoes and fish stock and stir well. Bring to a boil, reduce the heat, cover, and simmer for 15 minutes. Uncover and simmer for 20–35 minutes, or until thickened.

Cut each red snapper in half, then add the fish pieces to the casserole, pushing them down into the liquid. Simmer the stew for an additional 5–6 minutes, or until the fish is just cooked.

Carefully stir in the olives, lemon, and fresh cilantro. Season to taste with salt and pepper and serve immediately with couscous.

GOAN-STYLE SEAFOOD CURRY

Heat the oil in a wok or large skillet over high heat. Add the mustard seeds and stir them around for about 1 minute, or until they jump. Stir in the curry leaves.

Add the shallots and garlic and stir for about 5 minutes, or until the shallots are golden. Stir in the turmeric, coriander, and chili powder and continue stirring for about 30 seconds.

Add the dissolved creamed coconut. Bring to a boil, then reduce the heat to medium and stir for about 2 minutes.

Reduce the heat to low, add the fish, and simmer for 1 minute, spooning the sauce over the fish and very gently stirring it around. Add the shrimp and continue to simmer for an additional 4–5 minutes until the fish flesh flakes easily and the shrimp turn pink and curl.

Add half the lime juice, then taste and add more lime juice and salt to taste. Sprinkle with the lime rind and serve with lime slices.

SERVES 4–6

3 tbsp vegetable oil or peanut oil

1 tbsp black mustard seeds

12 fresh curry leaves or 1 tbsp dried

6 shallots, finely chopped

1 garlic clove, crushed

1 tsp ground turmeric

½ ground coriander

¼–½ tsp chili powder

5 oz/140 g creamed coconut, grated and dissolved in 1¼ cups boiling water

1 lb 2 oz/500 g skinless, boneless white fish, such as monkfish or cod, cut into large chunks

1 lb/450 g large raw shrimp, shelled and deveined

juice and finely grated rind of 1 lime

salt

lime slices, to serve

VEGETABLES

RATATOUILLE

SERVES 4

Coarsely chop the eggplants and zucchini, and seed and chop the bell peppers. Slice the onions and finely chop the garlic. Heat the oil in a large skillet. Add the onions and cook over low heat, stirring occasionally, for 5 minutes, or until softened. Add the garlic and cook, stirring frequently for an additional 2 minutes.

Add the eggplants, zucchini, and bell peppers. Increase the heat to medium and cook, stirring occasionally, until the bell peppers begin to color. Add the bouquet garni, reduce the heat, cover, and simmer gently for 40 minutes.

Stir in the chopped tomatoes and season to taste with salt and pepper. Re-cover the pan and simmer gently for an additional 10 minutes. Remove and discard the bouquet garni. Serve warm or cold.

- 2 medium-size eggplants
- 4 zucchini
- 2 yellow bell peppers
- 2 red bell peppers
- 2 onions
- 2 garlic cloves
- ⅔ cup olive oil
- 1 bouquet garni
- 3 large tomatoes, peeled, seeded, and coarsely chopped

salt and pepper

ROASTED SUMMER VEGETABLES

Brush an ovenproof dish with a little oil. Arrange the fennel, onions, tomatoes, eggplant, zucchini, and bell peppers in the dish and tuck the garlic cloves and rosemary sprigs among them. Drizzle with the remaining oil and season to taste with pepper.

Roast the vegetables in a preheated oven, 400°F/200°C, for 10 minutes. Turn the vegetables over, return the dish to the oven, and roast for an additional 10–15 minutes or until the vegetables are tender and beginning to turn golden brown.

Serve the vegetables straight from the dish or transfer to a warm serving platter. Serve immediately, with crusty bread, if using, to soak up the juices.

SERVES 4

2 tbsp olive oil

1 fennel bulb, cut into wedges

2 red onions, cut into wedges

2 beefsteak tomatoes, cut into wedges

1 eggplant, thickly sliced

2 zucchini, thickly sliced

1 yellow bell pepper, seeded and cut into chunks

1 red bell pepper, seeded and cut into chunks

1 orange bell pepper, seeded and cut into chunks

4 garlic cloves

4 fresh rosemary sprigs

ground black pepper

crusty bread, to serve (optional)

POTATO &
MUSHROOM PIE

SERVES 4

2 tbsp butter

1 lb/450 g waxy potatoes, thinly sliced and parboiled

2 cups sliced mixed mushrooms

1 tbsp chopped rosemary

4 tbsp snipped chives, plus extra to garnish

2 garlic cloves, crushed

²⁄₃ cup heavy cream

salt and pepper

Grease a shallow round ovenproof dish with butter.

Layer a quarter of the potatoes in the bottom of the dish. Arrange a quarter of the mushrooms on top of the potatoes and sprinkle with a quarter of the rosemary, chives, and garlic. Continue making layers in the same order, finishing with a layer of potatoes on top.

Pour the heavy cream over the top of the potatoes. Season to taste with salt and pepper.

Cook in a preheated oven, 375°F/190°C, for about 45 minutes or until the pie is golden brown on top and piping hot.

Garnish with snipped chives and serve at once straight from the dish.

EGGPLANT GRATIN

Heat the oil in a flameproof casserole over medium heat. Add the onions and cook for 5 minutes or until soft. Add the garlic and cook for a few seconds or until just beginning to color. Using a slotted spoon, transfer the onion mixture to a plate.

Cook the eggplant slices in batches in the same flameproof casserole until they are just lightly browned. Transfer to another plate.

Preheat the oven to 400°F/200°C. Arrange a layer of eggplant slices in the bottom of the casserole dish. Sprinkle with the parsley, thyme, and salt and pepper.

Add a layer of onion, tomatoes, and mozzarella, sprinkling parsley, thyme, and salt and pepper over each layer.

Continue layering, finishing with a layer of eggplant slices. Sprinkle with the Parmesan. Bake, uncovered, for 20–30 minutes or until the top is golden and the eggplants are tender. Serve hot.

SERVES 2

4 tbsp olive oil

2 onions, finely chopped

2 garlic cloves, very finely chopped

2 eggplants, thickly sliced

3 tbsp fresh flat-leaf parsley, chopped

½ tsp dried thyme

14 oz/400 g canned chopped tomatoes

1½ cups coarsely grated mozzarella

6 tbsp freshly grated Parmesan

salt and pepper

PARMESAN RISOTTO WITH MUSHROOMS

Heat the oil in a large, deep skillet. Add the rice and cook over low heat, stirring constantly, for 2–3 minutes, until the grains are thoroughly coated in oil and translucent.

Add the garlic, onion, celery, and bell pepper and cook, stirring frequently, for 5 minutes. Add the mushrooms and cook for 3–4 minutes. Stir in the oregano.

Gradually add the hot stock, a ladleful at a time. Stir constantly and add more liquid as the rice absorbs each addition. Increase the heat to medium so that the liquid bubbles. Cook for 20 minutes, or until all the liquid is absorbed and the rice is creamy. Add the sun-dried tomatoes, if using, 5 minutes before the end of the cooking time, then season to taste with salt and pepper.

Remove the risotto from the heat and stir in half the Parmesan until it melts. Transfer the risotto to warmed bowls. Top with the remaining cheese, garnish with flat-leaf parsley or bay leaves, and serve at once.

SERVES 6

2 tbsp olive oil or vegetable oil

generous 1 cup risotto rice

2 garlic cloves, crushed

1 onion, chopped

2 celery stalks, chopped

1 red or green bell pepper, seeded and chopped

8 oz/225 g button mushrooms, thinly sliced

1 tbsp chopped fresh oregano or 1 tsp dried oregano

4 cups boiling vegetable stock

¼ cup sun-dried tomatoes in olive oil, drained and chopped (optional)

½ cup finely grated Parmesan cheese

salt and pepper

fresh flat-leaf parsley sprigs or bay leaves, to garnish

RISOTTO WITH ARTICHOKE HEARTS

SERVES 4

8 oz/225 g canned artichoke hearts

1 tbsp olive oil

3 tbsp butter

1 small onion, finely chopped

scant 1½ cups risotto rice

5 cups boiling vegetable stock

¾ cup freshly grated Parmesan or Grana Padano cheese

salt and pepper

fresh flat-leaf parsley sprigs, to garnish

Drain the artichoke hearts, reserving the liquid, and cut them into quarters.

Heat the oil with 2 tablespoons of the butter in a large, deep skillet over medium heat until the butter has melted. Stir in the onion and cook gently, stirring occasionally, for 5 minutes, or until soft and starting to turn golden. Do not brown.

Add the rice and mix to coat in oil and butter. Cook, stirring constantly, for 2–3 minutes, or until the grains are translucent.

Gradually add the artichoke liquid and the hot stock, a ladleful at a time. Stir constantly and add more liquid as the rice absorbs each addition. Increase the heat to medium so that the liquid bubbles. Cook for 15 minutes, then add the artichoke hearts. Cook for an additional 5 minutes, or until all the liquid is absorbed and the rice is creamy. Season to taste.

Remove the risotto from the heat and add the remaining butter. Mix well, then stir in the Parmesan until it melts. Season, if necessary. Spoon the risotto into warmed bowls, garnish with parsley sprigs, and serve at once.

VEGETARIAN PAELLA

Put the saffron threads and water in a small bowl or cup and let infuse for a few minutes.

Meanwhile, heat the oil in a paella pan or wide, shallow skillet and cook the onion over medium heat, stirring, for 2–3 minutes, or until softened. Add the garlic, bell peppers, and eggplant and cook, stirring frequently, for 5 minutes.

Add the rice and cook, stirring constantly, for 1 minute, or until glossy and coated. Pour in the stock and add the tomatoes, saffron and its soaking water, and salt and pepper to taste. Bring to a boil, then reduce the heat and let simmer, shaking the skillet frequently and stirring occasionally, for 15 minutes.

Stir in the mushrooms, green beans, and pinto beans with their can juices. Cook for an additional 10 minutes, then serve immediately.

SERVES 4–6

½ tsp saffron threads

2 tbsp hot water

6 tbsp olive oil

1 Spanish onion, sliced

3 garlic cloves, minced

1 red bell pepper, seeded and sliced

1 orange bell pepper, seeded and sliced

1 large eggplant, cubed

1 cup medium-grain paella rice

2½ cups vegetable stock

1 lb/450 g tomatoes, peeled and chopped

4 oz/115 g button mushrooms, sliced

4 oz/115 g green beans, halved

14 oz/400 g canned pinto beans

salt and pepper

EGG-FRIED RICE WITH VEGETABLES

If you wish to make the crispy onion topping, heat the oil in a large wok or skillet and sauté the onions until crispy and brown. Remove from the pan and keep warm.

To make the rice, heat the oil in a wok or large skillet and sauté the garlic and chiles for 2–3 minutes. Add the mushrooms, snow peas, and corn, and stir-fry for 2–3 minutes before adding the soy sauce, sugar, and basil. Stir in the rice.

Push the mixture to one side of the wok and add the eggs to the bottom. Stir until lightly set before combining into the rice mixture. Serve immediately, topped with the crispy onions if using.

SERVES 4

2 tbsp vegetable oil or peanut oil

2 garlic cloves, finely chopped

2 fresh red chiles, seeded and chopped

4 oz/115 g button mushrooms, sliced

2 oz/55 g snow peas, halved

2 oz/55 g baby corn, halved

3 tbsp Thai soy sauce

1 tbsp light brown sugar

a few Thai basil leaves

3 cups rice, cooked and cooled

2 eggs, beaten

crispy onion topping (optional)

2 tbsp vegetable oil or peanut oil

2 onions, sliced

SPICED
BASMATI PILAU

SERVES 4

2½ cups basmati rice

6 oz/175 g broccoli, trimmed

6 tbsp vegetable oil

2 large onions, chopped

8 oz/225 g button mushrooms, sliced

2 garlic cloves, crushed

6 cardamom pods, split

6 whole cloves

8 black peppercorns

1 cinnamon stick or piece of cassia bark

1 tsp ground turmeric

5 cups boiling vegetable stock or water

⅓ cup seedless raisins

½ cup unsalted pistachios, coarsely chopped

salt and pepper

Place the rice in a strainer and wash well under cold running water. Drain. Trim off most of the broccoli stalk, then quarter the stalk lengthwise and cut diagonally into 1-cm/½-inch pieces. Cut the remaining broccoli into small florets.

Heat the oil in a large skillet. Add the onions and broccoli stalks and cook over low heat, stirring frequently, for 3 minutes. Add the mushrooms, rice, garlic, and spices and cook for 1 minute, stirring, until the rice is coated in oil.

Add the boiling stock and season to taste with salt and pepper. Stir in the broccoli florets and return the mixture to a boil. Cover, reduce the heat, and cook over low heat for 15 minutes without uncovering the pan.

Remove the pan from the heat and let the pilau stand for 5 minutes without uncovering. Remove the whole spices, add the raisins and pistachios, and gently fork through to fluff up the grains. Serve the pilau hot.

MOROCCAN STScrollView

MOROCCAN STEW

Heat the oil in a large, heavy-bottom pan with a tight-fitting lid, and cook the onion, garlic, chile, and eggplant, stirring frequently, for 5–8 minutes, or until softened.

Add the cumin, coriander, and saffron and cook, stirring constantly, for 2 minutes. Bruise the cinnamon stick.

Add the cinnamon, squash, sweet potatoes, prunes, stock, and tomatoes to the pan and bring to a boil. Reduce the heat, then cover and simmer, stirring occasionally, for 20 minutes. Add the chickpeas to the pan and cook for an additional 10 minutes. Discard the cinnamon and serve garnished with the fresh cilantro.

SERVES 4

- 2 tbsp olive oil
- 1 red onion, finely chopped
- 2–4 garlic cloves, crushed
- 1 fresh red chile, seeded and sliced
- 1 eggplant, about 8 oz/225 g, cut into small chunks
- 1 tsp ground cumin
- 1 tsp ground coriander
- pinch of saffron threads
- 1–2 cinnamon sticks
- ½–1 butternut squash, about 1 lb/450 g, peeled, seeded, and cut into small chunks
- 8 oz/225 g sweet potatoes, cut into small chunks
- scant ½ cup prunes
- 2–2½ cups vegetable stock
- 4 tomatoes, chopped
- 14 oz/400 g canned chickpeas, drained and rinsed
- 1 tbsp chopped fresh cilantro, to garnish

POTATO & LEMON CASSEROLE

Heat the olive oil in a flameproof casserole. Add the onions and sauté over medium heat, stirring frequently, for 3 minutes.

Add the garlic and cook for 30 seconds. Stir in the ground cumin, ground coriander, and cayenne and cook, stirring constantly, for 1 minute.

Add the carrot, turnips, zucchini, and potatoes and stir to coat in the oil.

Add the lemon juice and rind and the vegetable stock. Season to taste with salt and pepper. Cover and cook over medium heat, stirring occasionally, for 20–30 minutes until tender.

Remove the lid, sprinkle in the chopped fresh cilantro and stir well. Serve immediately.

SERVES 4

scant ½ cup olive oil

2 red onions, cut into 8 wedges

3 garlic cloves, crushed

2 tsp ground cumin

2 tsp ground coriander

pinch of cayenne pepper

1 carrot, thickly sliced

2 small turnips, quartered

1 zucchini, sliced

1 lb 2 oz/500 g potatoes, thickly sliced

juice and grated rind of 2 large lemons

1¼ cups vegetable stock

2 tbsp chopped fresh cilantro

salt and pepper

LENTIL & RICE CASSEROLE

SERVES 4

1 cup red lentils

generous ¼ cup long-grain rice

5 cups vegetable stock

1 leek, cut into chunks

3 garlic cloves, crushed

14 oz/400 g canned chopped tomatoes

1 tsp ground cumin

1 tsp chili powder

1 tsp garam masala

1 red bell pepper, seeded and sliced

3½ oz/100 g small broccoli florets

8 baby corn, halved lengthwise

2 oz/55 g green beans, halved

1 tbsp shredded fresh basil

salt and pepper

fresh basil sprigs, to garnish

Place the lentils, rice, and vegetable stock in a large, flameproof casserole and cook over low heat, stirring occasionally, for 20 minutes.

Add the leek, garlic, tomatoes and their can juice, ground cumin, chili powder, garam masala, sliced bell pepper, broccoli, baby corn, and green beans to the casserole.

Bring the mixture to a boil, reduce the heat, cover, and simmer for an additional 10–15 minutes or until all the vegetables are tender.

Add the shredded basil and season with salt and pepper to taste.

Garnish with fresh basil sprigs and serve immediately.

VEGETABLE GOULASH

Put the sun-dried tomatoes in a small heatproof bowl, then cover with almost boiling water and let soak for 15–20 minutes. Drain, reserving the soaking liquid.

Heat the oil in a large, heavy-bottom pan, with a tight-fitting lid, and cook the chiles, garlic, and vegetables, stirring frequently, for 5–8 minutes, or until softened. Blend the tomato paste with a little of the stock in a pitcher and pour over the vegetable mixture, then add the remaining stock, lentils, the sun-dried tomatoes and their soaking liquid, and the paprika and thyme.

Bring to a boil, then reduce the heat and simmer, covered, for 15 minutes. Add the fresh tomatoes and simmer for an additional 15 minutes, or until the vegetables and lentils are tender. Serve topped with spoonfuls of sour cream, accompanied by crusty bread.

SERVES 4

¼ cup sun-dried tomatoes, chopped

2 tbsp olive oil

½–1 tsp crushed dried chiles

2–3 garlic cloves, chopped

1 large onion, cut into small wedges

1 small celery root, cut into small chunks

8 oz/225 g carrots, sliced

8 oz/225 g new potatoes, scrubbed and cut into chunks

1 small acorn squash, seeded, peeled, and cut into small chunks, about 8 oz/225 g prepared weight

2 tbsp tomato paste

1¼ cups vegetable stock

2½ cups canned Puy or green lentils, drained and rinsed

1–2 tsp hot paprika

few fresh sprigs of thyme

1 lb/450 g ripe tomatoes

sour cream

crusty bread, to serve

RIBOLLITA

Heat the oil in a large saucepan and cook the onions, carrots, and celery for 10–15 minutes, stirring frequently. Add the garlic, thyme, and salt and pepper to taste. Continue to cook for an additional 1–2 minutes, until the vegetables are golden and caramelized.

Add the cannellini beans to the pan and pour in the tomatoes. Add enough of the water to cover the vegetables.

Bring to a boil and simmer for 20 minutes. Add the parsley and Tuscan kale and cook for an additional 5 minutes.

Stir in the bread and add a little more water, if needed. The soup should be thick.

Taste and adjust the seasoning, if needed. Ladle into warmed serving bowls and serve hot, drizzled with extra virgin olive oil.

SERVES 4

3 tbsp olive oil

2 medium red onions, coarsely chopped

3 carrots, sliced

3 celery stalks, coarsely chopped

3 garlic cloves, chopped

1 tbsp chopped fresh thyme

14 oz/400 g canned cannellini beans, drained and rinsed

14 oz/400 g canned chopped tomatoes

2½ cups water or vegetable stock

2 tbsp chopped fresh parsley

1 lb 2 oz/500 g Tuscan kale or Savoy cabbage, trimmed and sliced

1 small day-old ciabatta loaf, torn into small pieces

salt and pepper

extra virgin olive oil, to serve

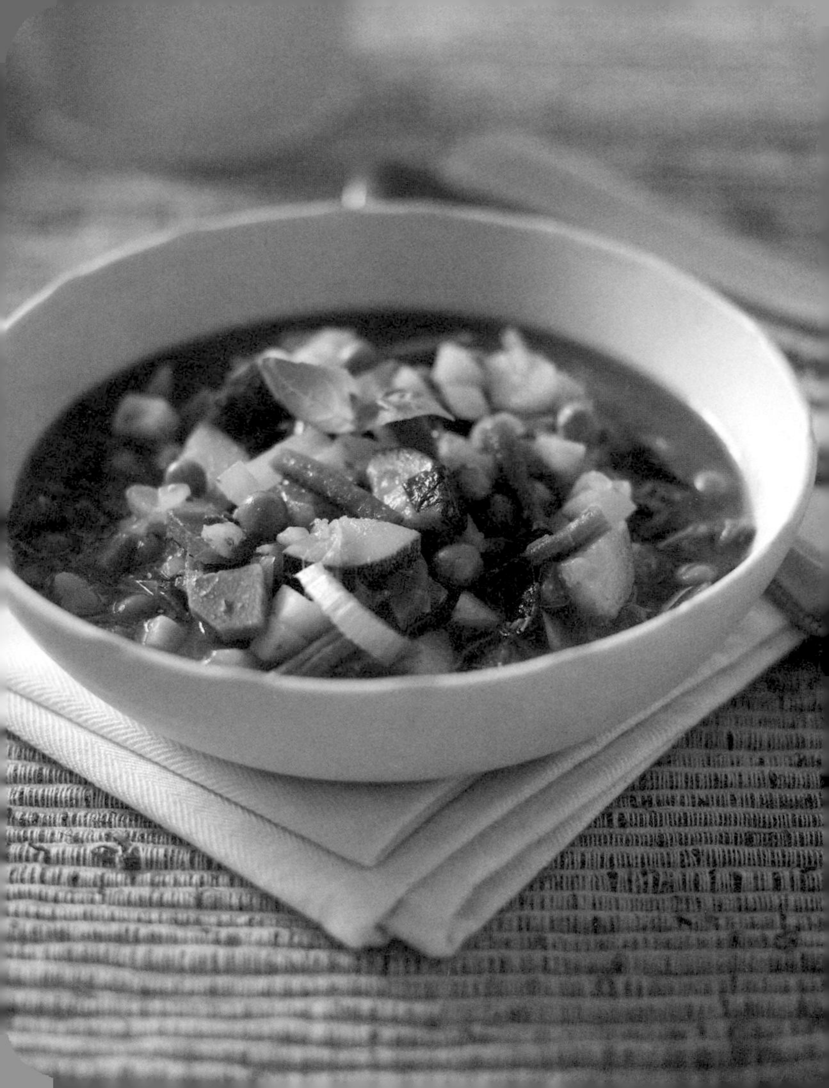

VEGETABLE STEW WITH PESTO

SERVES 6

1 tbsp olive oil

1 onion, finely chopped

1 large leek, thinly sliced

1 celery stalk, thinly sliced

1 carrot, quartered and thinly sliced

1 garlic clove, finely chopped

6¼ cups water

1 potato, diced

1 parsnip, finely diced

1 small kohlrabi or turnip, diced

5½ oz/150 g green beans, cut into small pieces

5½ oz/150 g fresh or frozen peas

2 small zucchini, quartered lengthwise and sliced

14 oz/400 g canned cannellini beans, drained and rinsed

3½ oz/100 g spinach leaves, cut into thin ribbons

3 tbsp prepared pesto

salt and pepper

Heat the olive oil in a large saucepan over medium–low heat. Add the onion and leek and cook for 5 minutes, stirring occasionally, until the onion softens. Add the celery, carrot, and garlic and cook, covered, for an additional 5 minutes, stirring frequently.

Add the water, potato, parsnip, kohlrabi, and green beans. Bring to a boil, reduce the heat to low, and simmer, covered, for 5 minutes.

Add the peas, zucchini, and cannellini beans, and season generously with salt and pepper. Cover again and simmer for about 25 minutes until all the vegetables are tender.

Add the spinach to the stew and simmer for an additional 5 minutes. Taste and adjust the seasoning and stir about a tablespoon of pesto into the stew. Ladle into warmed bowls and serve with the remaining pesto.

VEGETABLE STEW WITH GREEN LENTILS

Heat the oil in a large saucepan over medium heat, add the onion, garlic, and carrot and cook for 3–4 minutes, stirring frequently, until the onion starts to soften. Add the cabbage and cook for an additional 2 minutes.

Add the tomatoes, thyme, and 1 bay leaf, then pour in the stock. Bring to a boil, reduce the heat to low, and cook gently, partially covered, for about 45 minutes until the vegetables are tender.

Meanwhile, put the lentils in another saucepan with the remaining bay leaf and the water. Bring just to a boil, reduce the heat, and simmer for about 25 minutes until tender. Drain off any remaining water, and set aside.

Let it cool slightly, then transfer to a food processor or blender and process until smooth, working in batches, if necessary. (If using a food processor, strain off the cooking liquid and reserve. Purée the soup solids with enough cooking liquid to moisten them, then combine with the remaining liquid.)

Return the stew to the saucepan and add the cooked lentils. Taste and add salt and pepper to taste, and cook for about 10 minutes to heat through. Ladle into warmed bowls and garnish with parsley.

SERVES 6

1 tbsp olive oil

1 onion, finely chopped

1 garlic clove, finely chopped

1 carrot, halved and thinly sliced

1 lb/450 g green cabbage, cored, quartered, and thinly sliced

14 oz/400 g canned chopped tomatoes

½ tsp dried thyme

2 bay leaves

6¼ cups chicken stock or vegetable stock

7 oz/200 g French green lentils

2 cups water

salt and pepper

chopped fresh parsley, to garnish

SPRING STEW

Heat the oil in a large, heavy-bottom pan with a tight-fitting lid, and cook the onions, celery, carrots, and potatoes, stirring frequently, for 5 minutes, or until softened. Add the stock, drained beans, bouquet garni, and soy sauce, then bring to a boil. Reduce the heat, then cover and simmer for 12 minutes.

Add the baby corn and fava beans and season to taste with salt and pepper. Simmer for an additional 3 minutes.

Meanwhile, discard the outer leaves and hard central core from the cabbage and shred the leaves. Add to the pan and simmer for an additional 3–5 minutes, or until all the vegetables are tender.

Blend the cornstarch with the water, then stir into the pan and cook, stirring, for 4–6 minutes, or until the liquid has thickened. Serve the cheese separately, for stirring into the stew.

SERVES 4

2 tbsp olive oil

4–8 baby onions, halved

1 celery stick, sliced

8 oz/225 g baby carrots, scrubbed and halved if large

10½ oz/300 g new potatoes, scrubbed and halved, or cut into quarters if large

3¾–5 cups vegetable stock

generous 2¾ cups canned cannellini beans, drained and rinsed

1 fresh bouquet garni

1½–2 tbsp light soy sauce

3 oz/85 g baby corn

1 cup frozen or shelled fresh fava beans, thawed if frozen

½–1 head of Savoy cabbage, about 8 oz/225 g

1½ tbsp cornstarch

2 tbsp cold water

salt and pepper

2–3 oz/55–85 g Parmesan or sharp Cheddar cheese, grated, to serve

CHILE BEAN STEW

SERVES 4–6

2 tbsp olive oil

1 onion, chopped

2–4 garlic cloves, chopped

2 fresh red chiles, seeded
 and sliced

1²/₃ cups canned kidney beans,
 drained and rinsed

1²/₃ cups canned cannellini beans,
 drained and rinsed

1²/₃ cups canned chickpeas,
 drained and rinsed

1 tbsp tomato paste

3–3³/₄ cups vegetable stock

1 red bell pepper, seeded
 and chopped

4 tomatoes, coarsely chopped

1¹/₂ cups frozen or shelled fresh
 fava beans, thawed if frozen

1 tbsp chopped fresh cilantro,
 plus extra to garnish

pepper

sour cream and a pinch of paprika,
 to garnish

Heat the oil in a large, heavy-bottom pan with a tight-fitting lid, and cook the onion, garlic, and chiles, stirring frequently, for 5 minutes, or until softened. Add the kidney beans, cannellini beans, and chickpeas. Blend the tomato paste with a little of the stock in a pitcher and pour over the bean mixture, then add the remaining stock. Bring to a boil, then reduce the heat and simmer for 10–15 minutes.

Add the red bell pepper, tomatoes, fava beans, and pepper to taste, and simmer for 15–20 minutes, or until all the vegetables are tender. Stir in the chopped cilantro

Garnish the stew with chopped cilantro and serve topped with spoonfuls of sour cream and a pinch of paprika.

VEGETABLES

257

TUSCAN BEAN STEW

Trim the fennel and reserve any feathery fronds, then cut the bulb into small strips. Heat the oil in a large, heavy-bottom pan with a tight-fitting lid, and cook the onion, garlic, chile, and fennel strips, stirring frequently, for 5–8 minutes, or until softened.

Add the eggplant and cook, stirring frequently, for 5 minutes. Blend the tomato paste with a little of the stock in a pitcher and pour over the fennel mixture, then add the remaining stock, and the tomatoes, vinegar, and oregano. Bring to a boil, then reduce the heat and simmer, covered, for 15 minutes, or until the tomatoes have begun to collapse.

Drain and rinse the beans, then drain again. Add them to the pan with the yellow bell pepper, zucchini, and olives. Simmer for an additional 15 minutes, or until the vegetables are tender. Taste and adjust the seasoning. Scatter with the Parmesan shavings and serve garnished with the reserved fennel fronds, accompanied by polenta wedges or crusty bread.

SERVES 4

1 large fennel bulb

2 tbsp olive oil

1 red onion, cut into small wedges

2–4 garlic cloves, sliced

1 fresh green chile, seeded and chopped

1 small eggplant, about 8 oz/ 225 g, cut into chunks

2 tbsp tomato paste

scant 2–2½ cups vegetable stock

1 lb/450 g ripe tomatoes

1 tbsp balsamic vinegar

a few sprigs of fresh oregano

14 oz/400 g canned borlotti beans

14 oz/400 g canned flageolets

1 yellow bell pepper, seeded and cut into small strips

1 zucchini, sliced into half moons

⅓ cup pitted black olives

1 oz/25 g Parmesan cheese, freshly shaved

salt and pepper

polenta wedges or crusty bread, to serve

KIDNEY BEAN, PUMPKIN & TOMATO STEW

Pick over the beans, cover generously with cold water, and set aside to soak for 6 hours or overnight. Drain the beans, put in a large saucepan, and add enough cold water to cover by 2 inches. Bring to a boil and simmer for 10 minutes. Drain and rinse well. Clean the saucepan.

Heat the oil in the cleaned saucepan over medium heat. Add the onions, cover, and cook for 3–4 minutes, until they are just softened, stirring occasionally. Add the garlic, celery, and carrot, and continue cooking for 2 minutes.

Add the water, drained beans, tomato paste, thyme, oregano, cumin, and bay leaf. When the mixture begins to bubble, reduce the heat to low. Cover and simmer gently for 1 hour, stirring occasionally.

Stir in the tomatoes, pumpkin, and chili paste and continue simmering for an additional hour, or until the beans and pumpkin are tender, stirring from time to time.

Season to taste with salt and pepper and stir in a little more chili paste, if desired. Ladle the soup into bowls, garnish with cilantro, and serve.

SERVES 4–6

9 oz/250 g dried kidney beans

1 tbsp olive oil

2 onions, finely chopped

4 garlic cloves, finely chopped

1 celery stalk, thinly sliced

1 carrot, halved and thinly sliced

5 cups water

2 tsp tomato paste

⅛ tsp dried thyme

⅛ tsp dried oregano

⅛ tsp ground cumin

1 bay leaf

14 oz/400 g canned chopped tomatoes

9 oz/250 g peeled pumpkin flesh, diced

¼ tsp chili paste, or to taste

salt and pepper

fresh cilantro, to garnish

BEANS & GREENS STEW

SERVES 4

9 oz/250 g dried cannellini beans

1 tbsp olive oil

2 onions, finely chopped

4 garlic cloves, finely chopped

1 celery stalk, thinly sliced

2 carrots, halved and thinly sliced

5 cups water

¼ tsp dried thyme

¼ tsp dried marjoram

1 bay leaf

4½ oz/125 g leafy greens, such as chard, mustard, spinach, and kale, washed

salt and pepper

Pick over the beans, cover generously with cold water, and set aside to soak for 6 hours or overnight. Drain the beans, put in a large saucepan, and add enough cold water to cover by 2 inches/ 5 cm. Bring to a boil and boil for 10 minutes. Drain and rinse well. Clean the saucepan.

Heat the oil in the cleaned saucepan over medium heat. Add the onions and cook, covered, for 3–4 minutes, stirring occasionally, until the onions are just softened. Add the garlic, celery, and carrots, and continue cooking for 2 minutes.

Add the water, drained beans, thyme, marjoram, and bay leaf. When the mixture begins to bubble, reduce the heat to low. Cover and simmer gently, stirring occasionally, for about 1¼ hours until the beans are tender. Season with salt and pepper.

Let the soup cool slightly, then transfer 2 cups to a food processor or blender. Process until smooth and recombine with the soup.

Using a handful at a time, cut the greens crosswise into thin ribbons, keeping tender leaves like spinach separate. Add the thicker leaves and cook gently, uncovered, for 10 minutes. Stir in any remaining greens and continue cooking for 5–10 minutes, until all the greens are tender.

Taste and adjust the seasoning, if necessary. Remove and discard the bay leaf. Ladle the soup into warmed bowls and serve.

HOT & SOUR NOODLES WITH BEAN CURD

Put the lime rind, garlic, and ginger into a large pan with the stock and bring to a boil. Reduce the heat and let simmer for 5 minutes. Remove the lime rind, garlic, and ginger with a slotted spoon and discard.

Meanwhile, heat the vegetable oil in a large skillet over high heat, add the bean curd and cook, turning frequently, until golden. Remove from the skillet and drain on paper towels.

Add the noodles, mushrooms, and chile to the stock and let simmer for 3 minutes. Add the bean curd, scallions, soy sauce, lime juice, rice wine, and sesame oil and briefly heat through.

Divide the soup among 4 warmed bowls, sprinkle over the cilantro, and serve at once.

SERVES 4

3 strips of rind and juice of 1 lime

2 garlic cloves, peeled

2 slices fresh ginger

4 cups chicken stock

1 tbsp vegetable oil

5½ oz/150 g firm bean curd (drained weight), cubed

7 oz/200 g dried fine egg noodles

3½ oz/100 g shiitake mushrooms, sliced

1 fresh red chile, seeded and sliced

4 scallions, sliced

1 tsp soy sauce

1 tsp Chinese rice wine

1 tsp sesame oil

chopped fresh cilantro, to garnish

DESSERTS

APPLE & BLACKBERRY CRUMBLE

Preheat the oven to 400°F/200°C.

Peel and core the apples and cut into chunks. Place in a bowl with the blackberries, sugar, and cinnamon and mix together, then transfer to an ovenproof baking dish.

To make the crumble topping, sift the self-rising flour into a bowl and stir in the whole wheat flour. Add the butter and rub it in with your fingertips until the mixture resembles fine breadcrumbs. Stir in the sugar.

Spread the crumble over the apples and bake in the preheated oven for 40–45 minutes, or until the apples are soft and the crumble is golden brown and crisp. Serve with cream.

SERVES 4

2 lb/900 g tart cooking apples, peeled and sliced

10½ oz/300 g blackberries, fresh or frozen

¼ cup brown sugar

1 tsp ground cinnamon

crumble topping

⅔ cup self-rising flour

⅔ cup whole wheat flour

½ cup unsalted butter

¼ cup raw brown sugar

light or heavy cream, to serve

RHUBARB CRUMBLE

Preheat the oven to 375°F/190°C.

Cut the rhubarb into 1-inch/2.5-cm lengths and put in an ovenproof dish with the superfine sugar and the orange rind and juice.

To make the crumble topping, sift the flour into a bowl. Rub in the butter with your fingertips until the mixture resembles fine breadcrumbs. Stir in the brown sugar and ginger. Spread evenly over the fruit and press down lightly with a fork.

Bake in the center of the preheated oven for 25–30 minutes until the crumble is golden brown.

Serve warm with cream, yogurt, or custard.

SERVES 6

2 lb/900 g rhubarb

½ cup superfine sugar

grated rind and juice of
 1 orange

crumble topping

scant 1⅝ cups all-purpose or
 whole wheat flour

½ cup unsalted butter, diced and
 chilled

½ cup light brown sugar

1 tsp ground ginger

cream, yogurt, or custard,
 to serve

APRICOT CRUMBLE

SERVES 6

generous ½ cup unsalted butter, plus extra for greasing

1 cup brown sugar

3 cups pitted and sliced fresh apricots

1 tsp ground cinnamon

crumble topping

1½ cups whole wheat flour

½ cup hazelnuts, toasted and finely chopped

light or heavy cream, to serve

Preheat the oven to 400°F/200°C.

Put 3 tablespoons of the butter and ¾ cup of the sugar in a saucepan and melt together, stirring, over low heat. Add the apricots and cinnamon, cover the saucepan, and simmer for 5 minutes.

To make the crumble topping, put the flour in a bowl and rub in the remaining butter with your fingertips until the mixture resembles fine breadcrumbs. Stir in the remaining sugar and then the hazelnuts.

Remove the fruit from the heat and arrange in the bottom of an ovenproof dish. Sprinkle the crumble topping evenly over the fruit until it is covered all over. Transfer to the preheated oven and bake for about 25 minutes, until golden. Remove from the oven and serve hot with cream.

APPLE & PLUM CRUMBLE

Preheat the oven to 350°F/180°C.

Mix the apples, plums, apple juice, and sugar together in a round pie dish.

To make the crumble topping, sift the flour into a mixing bowl and rub in the margarine with your fingertips until it resembles fine breadcrumbs. Stir in the buckwheat and rice flakes, sunflower seeds, sugar, and cinnamon, then spoon the topping over the fruit in the dish.

Bake the crumble in the preheated oven for 30–35 minutes, or until the topping is lightly browned and crisp. Serve with cream.

SERVES 4

4 apples, peeled, cored, and diced

5 plums, halved, pitted, and quartered

4 tbsp fresh apple juice

1 oz/25 g light brown sugar

crumble topping

4 oz/115 g all-purpose flour

6 tbsp margarine, diced

1 oz/25 g buckwheat flakes

1 oz/25 g rice flakes

1 oz/25 g sunflower seeds

1¾ oz/50 g light brown sugar

¼ tsp ground cinnamon

light or heavy cream, to serve

PEAR & TOFFEE DESSERT

Preheat the oven to 400°F/200°C.

To make the crumble topping, put the flour in a large, heatproof dish and rub in the butter with your fingertips until the mixture resembles fine breadcrumbs. Stir in 4 tablespoons of the sugar and the chopped hazelnuts, then cook in the preheated oven for 5–10 minutes until heated through.

To make the toffee, put the dark corn syrup into a saucepan over low heat. Add the sugar, 1 tablespoon of the butter, and all the cream and vanilla extract, and bring gently to a boil. Simmer for 3 minutes, stirring constantly, then remove from the heat and set aside.

Put the remaining butter in a skillet and melt over low heat. Meanwhile, peel and coarsely chop the pears, then add them to the skillet and cook, stirring gently, for 3 minutes. Stir in the toffee and continue to cook, stirring, over low heat for another 3 minutes.

Transfer the pear-and-toffee mixture to an ovenproof pie dish. Arrange the crumble evenly over the top, then sprinkle over the remaining sugar and dot with the last tablespoon of butter. Bake in the preheated oven for 25–30 minutes or until the crumble is golden brown. Remove from the oven and serve with vanilla ice cream.

SERVES 4

4 large pears
1 tbsp unsalted butter
vanilla ice cream, to serve

crumble topping
¾ cup self-rising flour
½ cup unsalted butter, diced
5 tbsp raw brown sugar
2 tbsp finely chopped hazelnuts

toffee
3 tbsp dark corn syrup
3 tbsp raw brown sugar
2 tbsp unsalted butter
2 tbsp light cream
½ tsp vanilla extract

SHERRIED NECTARINE DESSERT

SERVES 4

6 nectarines

1 oz/25 g raw brown sugar

2 tbsp sweet sherry

light or heavy cream, to serve

crumble topping

1¼ cups all-purpose flour

¼ cup raw brown sugar, plus extra
   for sprinkling

½ cup unsalted butter, melted

Preheat the oven to 400°F/200°C.

Using a sharp knife, halve the nectarines, remove and discard the pits, then cut the flesh into fairly thick slices. Put the nectarine slices into an ovenproof dish, sprinkle over the sugar and sweet sherry, then cook in the preheated oven for 5–10 minutes until heated through.

To make the crumble topping, put the flour and sugar in a large bowl, then quickly mix in the melted butter until crumbly. Carefully arrange the crumble over the nectarines in an even layer—keep your touch light or the crumble will sink into the filling and get mushy. Scatter a little more sugar over the top, then transfer to the preheated oven and bake for 25–30 minutes or until the crumble topping is golden brown.

Remove from the oven and serve with generous spoonfuls of cream.

GOOSEBERRY & PISTACHIO DESSERT

Preheat the oven to 400°F/200°C.

Put the gooseberries in an ovenproof dish, pour over the honey, and cook in the preheated oven for 5–10 minutes until heated through.

Put the superfine sugar, orange juice, orange zest, and water in a small saucepan, then bring to a boil, stirring, over medium heat. Reduce the heat and simmer for 5 minutes, then remove from the heat and set aside to cool.

Meanwhile, to make the crumble topping, put the flour in a bowl, then rub in the butter with your fingertips until the mixture resembles fine breadcrumbs. Now stir in 4 tablespoons of the raw brown sugar and the pistachios.

Pour the cooled orange syrup over the gooseberries, then lightly sprinkle over the crumble mixture in an even layer. Do not press the crumble into the syrup or it will become mushy. Sprinkle over the remaining raw brown sugar.

Bake in the preheated oven for 25–30 minutes or until the crumble topping is golden brown. Remove from the oven and serve with vanilla- or orange-flavored ice cream.

SERVES 4

14 oz/400 g gooseberries
1 tbsp honey
½ cup superfine sugar
1 tbsp orange juice
1 tbsp grated orange zest
6 tbsp water
grated orange zest, to decorate
vanilla- or orange-flavored ice cream, to serve

crumble topping
¾ cup self-rising flour
½ cup unsalted butter, diced
5 tbsp raw brown sugar
1¾ oz/50 g pistachios, finely chopped

PRUNE DESSERT
WITH ALLSPICE

Put the prunes and golden raisins in a large bowl, cover with the water, and let soak overnight or for at least 8 hours.

Preheat the oven to 350°F/180°C. Drain the fruit but reserve the soaking liquid. Put the fruit in a large saucepan with the sugar and 2½ cups of the soaking liquid. Bring to a boil, then reduce the heat and simmer for about 10 minutes, or until the fruit has softened.

Meanwhile, to make the crumble topping, put the flour and allspice in a bowl, then rub in the butter with your fingertips until the mixture resembles fine breadcrumbs. Now stir in 4 tablespoons of the raw brown sugar.

Remove the fruit from the heat, stir in the allspice, and the rum if using, then pour into an ovenproof saucepan. Carefully arrange the crumble over the fruit in an even layer—keep your touch light or the crumble will sink into the filling and get mushy. Scatter the remaining sugar over the top, then transfer to the preheated oven and bake for 25 minutes, or until the crumble topping is golden brown.

Remove from the oven and serve with cream.

SERVES 4

8 oz/225 g prunes, chopped

8 oz/225 g golden raisins

3 cups water

3 tbsp raw brown sugar

1 tsp allspice

1 tbsp dark rum (optional)

light or heavy cream, to serve

crumble topping

¾ cup self-rising flour

½ tsp allspice

½ cup unsalted butter, diced

5 tbsp raw brown sugar

FRUIT COBBLER

SERVES 6

2 lb/900 g fresh berries and currants, such as blackberries, blueberries, raspberries, red currants, and black currants

½ cup superfine sugar

2 tbsp cornstarch

light or heavy cream, to serve

cobbler topping

1⅓ cups all-purpose flour

2 tsp baking powder

pinch of salt

4 tbsp unsalted butter, diced and chilled

2 tbsp superfine sugar

¾ cup buttermilk

1 tbsp raw brown sugar

Preheat the oven to 400°F/200°C.

Pick over the fruit, then mix with the superfine sugar and cornstarch and put in a 10-inch/25-cm shallow, ovenproof dish.

To make the cobbler topping, sift the flour, baking powder, and salt into a large bowl. Rub in the butter with your fingertips until the mixture resembles fine breadcrumbs, then stir in the superfine sugar. Pour in the buttermilk and mix to a soft dough.

Drop spoonfuls of the dough on top of the fruit roughly, so that it doesn't completely cover the fruit. Sprinkle with the raw brown sugar and bake in the preheated oven for 25-30 minutes, or until the crust is golden and the fruit is tender.

Remove from the oven and set aside for a few minutes before serving with cream.

PEACH COBBLER

Preheat the oven to 425°F/220°C.

Put the peaches into an ovenproof dish that is also suitable for serving. Add the sugar, lemon juice, cornstarch, and almond extract, and toss together. Bake the peaches in the oven for 20 minutes.

Meanwhile, to make the cobbler topping, sift the flour, all but 2 tablespoons of the sugar, the baking powder, and salt into a bowl. Rub in the butter with your fingertips until the mixture resembles fine breadcrumbs. Combine the egg and 5 tablespoons of the milk in a pitcher and mix into the dry ingredients with a fork until a soft, sticky dough forms. If the dough seems dry, stir in the extra tablespoon of milk.

Reduce the oven temperature to 400°F/200°C. Remove the peaches from the oven and drop spoonfuls of the topping over the surface, without smoothing. Sprinkle with the remaining sugar, return to the oven, and bake for an additional 15 minutes, or until the topping is golden brown and firm—the topping will spread as it cooks.

Serve hot or at room temperature with ice cream on the side.

SERVES 4–6

6 peaches, peeled and sliced

4 tbsp superfine sugar

½ tbsp lemon juice

1½ tsp cornstarch

½ tsp almond or vanilla extract

vanilla or butter pecan
   ice cream, to serve

cobbler topping

1¼ cups all-purpose flour

½ cup superfine sugar

1½ tsp baking powder

½ tsp salt

6 tbsp unsalted butter, diced

1 egg

5–6 tbsp milk

STRAWBERRY CREAM COBBLER

Preheat the oven to 400°F/200°C.

Arrange the strawberries evenly in the bottom of an ovenproof dish, then sprinkle over the sugar and cook in the preheated oven for 5–10 minutes until heated through.

To make the cobbler topping, sift the flour and salt into a large mixing bowl. Rub in the butter with your fingertips until the mixture resembles fine breadcrumbs, then stir in the sugar. Add the beaten egg, then the golden raisins and raisins and mix lightly until incorporated. Stir in enough of the milk to make a smooth dough. Transfer to a clean, lightly floured board, knead lightly, then roll out to a thickness of about ½ inch/1 cm. Cut out circles using a 2-inch/5-cm cookie cutter. Arrange the dough circles over the strawberries, then brush the tops with a little milk.

Bake in the preheated oven for 25–30 minutes, or until the cobbler topping has risen and is lightly golden. Remove from the oven and serve with whipped heavy cream.

SERVES 4

1 lb 12 oz/800 g strawberries, hulled and halved

¼ cup superfine sugar

whipped heavy cream, to serve

cobbler topping

1½ cups self-rising flour, plus extra for dusting

pinch of salt

3 tbsp unsalted butter

2 tbsp superfine sugar

1 egg, beaten

1 oz/25 g golden raisins

1 oz/25 g raisins

5 tbsp milk, plus extra for glazing

SPICED MANGO & BLUEBERRY COBBLER

SERVES 4

2 ripe mangoes, pitted and cut
into fairly thick slices

9 oz/250 g blueberries

½ tsp grated nutmeg

1 tbsp lime juice

¼ cup superfine sugar,
or to taste

heavy cream, to serve

cobbler topping

1½ cups self-rising flour, plus
extra for dusting

pinch of salt

½ tsp cinnamon

3 tbsp unsalted butter

2 tbsp superfine sugar

3 tbsp dried blueberries
(optional)

1 egg, beaten

5 tbsp milk, plus extra
for glazing

Preheat the oven to 400°F/200°C.

Put the mangoes and blueberries in the bottom of an ovenproof saucepan, then sprinkle over the nutmeg, lime juice, and superfine sugar and cook in the preheated oven for 5–10 minutes until heated through.

To make the cobbler topping, sift the flour, salt, and cinnamon into a large mixing bowl. Rub in the butter with your fingertips until the mixture resembles fine breadcrumbs, then mix in the sugar and the dried blueberries if using. Add the beaten egg, then stir in enough of the milk to make a smooth dough. Transfer to a clean, lightly floured board, knead lightly, then roll out to a thickness of about ½ inch/1 cm. Cut out circles using a 2-inch/5-cm cookie cutter. Arrange the dough circles over the fruit, then brush the tops with a little milk.

Bake in the preheated oven for 25–30 minutes, or until the cobbler topping has risen and is lightly golden. Remove from the oven and serve with heavy cream.

CHOCOLATE BROWNIES

Preheat the oven to 350°F/180°C. Grease and line an 11 x 7-inch/
28 x 18-cm rectangular cake pan with parchment paper.

Put the butter and chopped dark chocolate into a heatproof
bowl and set over a saucepan of simmering water until melted.
Remove from the heat. Sift the flour into a large bowl, add the
sugar, and mix well. Stir the eggs into the chocolate mixture then
beat into the flour mixture. Add the nuts, golden raisins, and
chocolate chips, and mix well. Spoon evenly into the cake pan
and level the surface.

Bake in the oven for 30 minutes, or until firm. To check whether
the cake is cooked through, insert a toothpick into the center—it
should come out clean. If not, return the cake to the oven for a
few minutes. Remove from the oven and let cool for 15 minutes.
Turn out onto a wire rack to cool completely. To decorate, drizzle
the melted white chocolate in fine lines over the cake, then cut
into bars or squares. Set aside to set before serving.

MAKES 15

8 oz/225 g unsalted butter, diced,
  plus extra for greasing

5½ oz/150 g dark chocolate,
  chopped

1½ cups all-purpose flour

1 cup dark brown sugar

4 eggs, beaten

¼ cup chopped blanched
  hazelnuts

½ cup golden raisins

½ cup dark chocolate chips

4 oz/115 g white chocolate,
  melted, to decorate

CHOCOLATE FUDGE BROWNIES

Preheat the oven to 350°F/180°C. Lightly grease an 8-inch/
20-cm square shallow cake pan and line the bottom with
parchment paper.

Beat together the cheese, vanilla extract, and 5 teaspoons of
superfine sugar until smooth, then set aside.

Beat the eggs and remaining superfine sugar together until
light and fluffy. Place the butter and unsweetened cocoa in a
small pan and heat gently, stirring until the butter melts and the
mixture combines, then stir it into the egg mixture. Fold in the
flour and nuts.

Pour half of the cake batter into the prepared pan and smooth
the top. Carefully spread the soft cheese over it, then cover it
with the remaining cake batter. Bake in the preheated oven for
40–45 minutes, then cool in the pan.

To make the frosting, melt the butter in the milk. Stir in the
confectioners' sugar and unsweetened cocoa. Spread the frosting
over the brownies and decorate with pecans (if using). Let the
frosting set, then cut into squares to serve.

MAKES 16

3 oz/85 g unsalted butter, plus
extra for greasing

scant 1 cup lowfat cream cheese

⅓ tsp vanilla extract

generous 1 cup superfine sugar

2 eggs

3 tbsp unsweetened cocoa

¾ cup self-rising flour, sifted

⅓ cup chopped pecans

fudge frosting
4 tbsp butter

1 tbsp milk

⅔ cup confectioners' sugar

2 tbsp unsweetened cocoa

pecans, to decorate (optional)

DOUBLE CHOCOLATE BROWNIES

MAKES 9 LARGE OR 16 SMALL

4 oz/115 g unsalted butter, plus extra for greasing

4 oz/115 g semisweet chocolate, broken into pieces

1⅓ cups superfine sugar

pinch of salt

1 tsp vanilla extract

2 large eggs

1 cup all-purpose flour

2 tbsp unsweetened cocoa

½ cup white chocolate chips

fudge sauce

4 tbsp unsalted butter

generous 1 cup superfine sugar

⅔ cup milk

generous 1 cup heavy cream

⅔ cup corn syrup

7 oz/200 g semisweet chocolate, broken into pieces

Preheat the oven to 350°F/180°C. Grease and line the bottom of a 7-inch/18-cm square cake pan with parchment paper.

Place the butter and chocolate in a small heatproof bowl set over a saucepan of gently simmering water until melted. Stir until smooth, then cool slightly. Stir in the sugar, salt, and vanilla extract. Add the eggs, one at a time, stirring well until blended.

Sift the flour and unsweetened cocoa into the cake batter and beat until smooth. Stir in the chocolate chips, then pour the batter into the prepared pan. Bake in the preheated oven for 35–40 minutes, or until the top is evenly colored and a skewer inserted into the center comes out almost clean. Let cool slightly while preparing the sauce.

To make the sauce, place the butter, sugar, milk, cream, and syrup in a small saucepan and heat gently until the sugar has dissolved. Bring to a boil and stir for 10 minutes, or until the mixture is caramel-colored. Remove from the heat and add the chocolate. Stir until smooth. Cut the brownies into squares and serve immediately with the sauce.

CAPPUCCINO BROWNIES

Preheat the oven to 350°F/180°C. Grease and line the bottom of a shallow 11 x 7-inch/28 x 18-cm cake pan with parchment paper.

Sift the flour, baking powder, and cocoa into a bowl, then add the butter, superfine sugar, eggs, and coffee. Beat well by hand or with an electric mixer until smooth, then spoon into the prepared pan and smooth the top.

Bake in the oven for 35–40 minutes, or until risen and firm. Cool in the pan for 10 minutes, then turn out onto a wire rack and peel off the lining paper. Cool completely.

To make the frosting, place the chocolate, butter, and milk in a bowl set over a saucepan of simmering water and stir until the chocolate has melted. Remove the bowl from the pan and sift in the confectioners' sugar. Beat until smooth, then spread over the cake. Dust the top of the cake with sifted cocoa, then cut into squares.

MAKES 15

8 oz/225 g unsalted butter, softened, plus extra for greasing

generous 1½ cups self-rising flour

1 tsp baking powder

1 tsp unsweetened cocoa, plus extra for dusting

generous 1 cup superfine sugar

4 eggs, beaten

3 tbsp instant coffee powder, dissolved in 2 tbsp hot water

fudge frosting

4 oz/115 g white chocolate, broken into pieces

2 oz/55 g butter, softened

3 tbsp milk

1¾ cups confectioners' sugar

UPSIDE-DOWN TOFFEE APPLE BROWNIES

Preheat the oven to 350°F/180°C. Grease a 9-inch/23-cm square shallow cake pan.

For the topping, place the sugar and remaining butter in a small saucepan and heat gently, stirring, until melted. Pour into the prepared cake pan. Arrange the apple slices on top.

For the brownies, place the butter and sugar in a bowl and beat well until pale and fluffy. Gradually beat in the eggs.

Sift together the flour, baking powder, baking soda, and spice and fold into the mixture. Stir in the apples and nuts.

Pour into the prepared cake pan and bake for 35–40 minutes until firm and golden. Cool in the pan for 10 minutes, then turn out upside down and cut into squares.

MAKES 9

toffee apple topping

2 oz/55 g unsalted butter, plus extra for greasing

generous ⅓ cup light brown sugar

1 apple, cored and thinly sliced

brownies

4 oz/115 g unsalted butter

¾ cup light brown sugar

2 eggs, beaten

1¾ cups all-purpose flour

1 tsp baking powder

½ tsp baking soda

1½ tsp apple pie spice

2 apples, peeled and coarsely grated

¾ cup chopped hazelnuts

CHOCOLATE MARSHMALLOW FINGERS

MAKES 18

12 oz/350 g graham crackers

4½ oz/125 g semisweet chocolate, broken into pieces

8 oz/225 g unsalted butter

2 tbsp superfine sugar

2 tbsp unsweetened cocoa

2 tbsp honey

⅔ cup mini marshmallows

½ cup white chocolate chips

Put the graham crackers in a plastic bag and, using a rolling pin, crush into small pieces.

Put the chocolate, butter, sugar, cocoa, and honey in a saucepan and heat gently until melted. Remove from the heat and cool slightly.

Stir the crushed crackers into the chocolate mixture until well mixed. Add the marshmallows and mix well then finally stir in the chocolate chips.

Turn the mixture into an 8-inch/20-cm square cake pan and lightly smooth the top. Put in the refrigerator and let chill for 2–3 hours until set. Cut into fingers before serving.

RICH VANILLA
ICE CREAM

Pour the light and heavy cream into a large, heavy-bottom saucepan. Split open the vanilla bean and scrape out the seeds into the cream, then add the whole vanilla bean. Bring almost to a boil, then remove from the heat and set aside for 30 minutes.

Put the egg yolks and sugar in a large bowl and whisk together until pale and the mixture leaves a trail when the whisk is lifted. Remove the vanilla bean from the cream, then slowly add the cream to the egg mixture, stirring all the time with a wooden spoon. Strain the mixture into the rinsed-out saucepan and cook over low heat for 10–15 minutes, stirring all the time, until the mixture thickens enough to coat the back of the spoon. Do not let the mixture boil or it will curdle. Remove the custard from the heat and cool for at least 1 hour, stirring from time to time to prevent a skin from forming.

If using an ice-cream machine, churn the cold custard in the machine following the manufacturer's instructions. Alternatively, freeze the custard in a freezerproof container, uncovered, for 1–2 hours or until it starts to set around the edges. Turn the custard into a bowl and stir with a fork or beat in a food processor until smooth. Return to the freezer and freeze for an additional 2–3 hours, or until firm or ready to serve. Cover the container with a lid for storing.

SERVES 4–6

1¼ cups light cream and
   1¼ cups heavy cream
1 vanilla bean
4 large egg yolks
generous ½ cup superfine sugar

CHOCOLATE ICE CREAM

Pour the milk into a large, heavy-bottom saucepan. Split open the vanilla bean and scrape out the seeds into the milk, then add the whole vanilla bean. Bring almost to a boil, then remove from the heat and set aside for 30 minutes. Remove the vanilla bean from the milk. Break the chocolate into the milk and heat gently, stirring constantly, until melted and smooth.

Put the egg yolks and sugar in a large bowl and whisk together until pale and the mixture leaves a trail when the whisk is lifted. Gradually add the chocolate mixture, stirring constantly with a wooden spoon. Strain the mixture into the rinsed-out saucepan and cook over low heat for 10–15 minutes, stirring constantly, until the mixture thickens enough to coat the back of a wooden spoon. Do not let the mixture boil or it will curdle. Remove the custard from the heat and let cool for at least 1 hour, stirring occasionally to prevent a skin from forming. Meanwhile, whip the cream until it holds its shape. Set aside in the refrigerator until ready to use.

If using an ice-cream machine, fold the whipped cream into the cold custard, then churn the mixture in the machine following the manufacturer's instructions. Alternatively, freeze the custard in a freezerproof container, uncovered, for 1–2 hours or until it begins to set around the edges. Turn the custard into a bowl and stir with a fork or beat in a food processor until smooth. Fold in the whipped cream. Return to the freezer and freeze for 2–3 hours more, or until firm or ready to serve. Cover the container with a lid for storing.

SERVES 4–6

1¼ cups milk

1 vanilla bean

3½ oz/100 g semisweet chocolate

3 egg yolks

scant ½ cup superfine sugar

1¼ cups heavy cream

BUTTERSCOTCH & PECAN ICE CREAM

SERVES 6

1¼ cups whole milk

4 tbsp butter

⅓ cup dark brown sugar

2 eggs

⅓ cup superfine sugar

1 tsp vanilla extract

1¼ cups heavy cream

scant 1 cup pecans, finely chopped

Pour the milk into a pan and bring almost to a boil. Remove from the heat. Melt the butter in a heavy pan, stir in the brown sugar, and heat gently until the sugar melts, then boil for 1 minute, or until beginning to caramelize, being careful not to let the mixture burn. Remove from the heat and gradually stir in the milk. Return to the heat and heat gently, stirring constantly, until well blended. Remove from the heat and let cool slightly. Put the eggs and superfine sugar in a large bowl and whisk together until pale. Gradually add the warm milk and vanilla extract, stirring constantly with a wooden spoon.

Strain the mixture into the rinsed-out saucepan and cook over low heat for 10–15 minutes, stirring constantly, until the mixture thickens enough to coat the back of the wooden spoon. Do not let the mixture boil or it will curdle. Remove the custard from the heat and let cool for at least 1 hour, stirring occasionally to prevent a skin from forming. Meanwhile, whip the cream until it holds its shape. Set aside in the refrigerator until ready to use.

If using an ice-cream machine, fold the whipped cream into the cold custard, then churn the mixture in the machine following the manufacturer's instructions. Just before the ice cream freezes, add the chopped pecans. Alternatively, freeze the custard in a freezerproof container, uncovered, for 1–2 hours or until it begins to set around the edges. Turn the custard into a bowl and stir with a fork or beat in a food processor until smooth. Fold in the whipped cream. Return to the freezer and freeze for 2–3 hours more, or until firm or ready to serve. Cover the container with a lid for storing. Keep in the freezer until ready to serve.

HONEYCOMB ICE CREAM

Grease a baking sheet with butter. Put the sugar and syrup in a heavy-bottom saucepan and heat gently until the sugar melts. Boil for 1–2 minutes, or until beginning to caramelize, being careful not to let the mixture burn. Stir in the baking soda, then immediately pour the mixture onto the prepared baking sheet but do not spread. Set aside to stand for about 10 minutes, until cold.

When the honeycomb is cold, put it into a strong plastic bag and crush into small pieces using a rolling pin or meat mallet. Whip the cream until it holds its shape, then whisk in the condensed milk.

If using an ice-cream machine, churn the mixture in the machine following the manufacturer's instructions. Just before the ice cream freezes, add the honeycomb pieces. Alternatively, freeze the custard in a freezerproof container, uncovered, for 1–2 hours or until it begins to set around the edges. Turn the custard into a bowl and stir with a fork or beat in a food processor until smooth. Fold in the honeycomb pieces. Return to the freezer and freeze for 2–3 hours more, or until firm or ready to serve. Cover the container with a lid for storing.

SERVES 6–8

unsalted butter, for greasing

scant ½ cup granulated sugar

2 tbsp light corn syrup

1 tsp baking soda

1¾ cups heavy cream

14 oz/400 g canned condensed milk

CAPPUCCINO ICE CREAM

SERVES 4

⅔ cup whole milk
2½ cups heavy cream
4 tbsp finely ground fresh coffee
3 large egg yolks
generous ½ cup superfine sugar
unsweetened cocoa, for dusting
chocolate-coated coffee beans,
  to decorate

Pour the milk and 2 cups of the cream into a heavy-bottom saucepan, stir in the coffee, and bring almost to a boil. Remove from the heat, set aside to stand for 5 minutes, then strain through a paper filter or a strainer lined with cheesecloth.

Put the egg yolks and sugar in a large bowl and whisk together until pale and the mixture leaves a trail when the whisk is lifted. Slowly add the milk mixture, stirring all the time with a wooden spoon. Strain the mixture into the rinsed-out heavy-bottom saucepan and cook over low heat for 10–15 minutes, stirring all the time, until the mixture thickens enough to coat the back of the spoon. Do not let the mixture boil or it will curdle. Remove the custard from the heat and let cool for at least 1 hour, stirring from time to time to prevent a skin from forming.

If using an ice-cream machine, churn the cold custard in the machine following the manufacturer's instructions. Alternatively, freeze the custard in a freezerproof container, uncovered, for 1–2 hours, or until it starts to set around the edges. Turn the custard into a bowl and stir with a fork or beat in a food processor until smooth. Return to the freezer and freeze for an additional 2–3 hours, or until firm or ready to serve. Cover the container with a lid for storing.

To serve, whip the remaining cream until it holds its shape. Scoop the ice cream into wide-brimmed coffee cups and smooth the tops. Spoon the whipped cream over the top of each and sprinkle with unsweetened cocoa. Decorate with chocolate-coated coffee beans.

CRUSHED CHERRY ICE CREAM

SERVES 6

½ cup sugar

⅔ cup water

1¼ cups fresh cherries, pitted, plus extra whole cherries to decorate

2 tbsp freshly squeezed orange juice

1¼ cups heavy cream

⅔ cup light cream

Put the sugar and water in a heavy-bottom saucepan and heat gently, stirring, until the sugar has dissolved, then bring to a boil and boil for 3 minutes. Reduce the heat, add the cherries, and let simmer gently for about 10 minutes, or until soft. Let the mixture cool for at least 1 hour.

When the cherries are cold, put them in a food processor or blender with the syrup. Add the orange juice and process the cherries until just coarsely chopped. Do not blend too much because the cherries should just be crushed, not pureed. Pour the heavy and light creams into a large bowl and whip together until the mixture holds its shape. Fold in the crushed cherries.

If using an ice-cream machine, churn the mixture in the machine following the manufacturer's instructions. Alternatively, freeze the mixture in a freezerproof container, uncovered, for 1–2 hours, or until it starts to set around the edges. Turn the mixture into a bowl and stir with a fork or beat in a food processor until smooth. Return to the freezer and freeze for an additional 2–3 hours, or until firm or ready to serve. Cover the container with a lid for storing. Serve decorated with whole cherries.

INDEX